ACCIDENTAL DEATH OF AN ANARCHIST

Dario Fo

AUTHORED by Kristin Sherwood
UPDATED AND REVISED by Christine McKeever

COVER DESIGN by Table XI Partners LLC
COVER PHOTO by Olivia Verma and © 2005 GradeSaver, LLC

BOOK DESIGN by Table XI Partners LLC

Published by GradeSaver LLC, www.gradesaver.com

First published in the United States of America by GradeSaver LLC. 2014

ISBN 978-1-60259-467-8

Printed in the United States of America

For other products and additional information please visit http://www.gradesaver.com

Table of Contents

Biography of Dario Fo (1926–) 1

Accidental Death of an Anarchist Summary 3

Accidental Death of an Anarchist Background 6

Accidental Death of an Anarchist Characters 9
- Bertozzo 9
- The Maniac 9
- Constables 10
- Inspector 10
- Superintendent 11
- Journalist 11

Accidental Death of an Anarchist Glossary 12
- all and sundry 12
- anyroad 12
- bash 12
- bog-standard 12
- boss-eyed 12
- cretinous 12
- drivel 12
- faff 12
- fob off 13
- give a toss 13
- gormless 13
- hoofer 13
- mickey-taking 13
- muck someone about 13
- ponce 13
- railway shunter 13
- rip the piss 13
- scuppered 14
- slag off 14
- sotto 14
- stitch up 14

take the piss 14
tetchy 14
top to tail 14
tosspot 14
Trappist 14
witter on 15
Tessa 15
ISA 15

Accidental Death of an Anarchist Themes 16
Reform versus Revolution 16
Fear and Submission 16
Corruption 17
Madness 17
Truth and Illusion 18
Layers of Reality 18
Class Oppression 19

Accidental Death of an Anarchist Quotes and Analysis 20

Accidental Death of an Anarchist Study Guide: Act One, Scene One Summary and Analysis 25

Accidental Death of an Anarchist Study Guide: Act One, Scene Two Summary and Analysis 28

Accidental Death of an Anarchist Study Guide: Act Two, Part 1 Summary and Analysis 33

Accidental Death of an Anarchist Study Guide: Act Two, Part 2 Summary and Analysis 36

Accidental Death of an Anarchist Symbols, Allegory and Motifs 40
the Maniac's false leg 40
the Maniac's false eye 40
the open window 40
the bomb 40
the tape recorder 41

Accidental Death of an Anarchist Metaphors and Similes 42
the Journalist as vulture 42

Bertozzo's slapstick 42
Switching the false hand for a woman's hand 42
the Maniac's disguises 43
insulting the Superintendent 43

Accidental Death of an Anarchist Irony 44
Irony for satire 44
Lying to reveal the truth 44
The Maniac's scandal 44

Accidental Death of an Anarchist Imagery 45
the open window 45
the Maniac's files 45
the exploding bomb 45

Accidental Death of an Anarchist Challenges of Translation 46

Accidental Death of an Anarchist Literary Elements 48

Accidental Death of an Anarchist Links 52

Accidental Death of an Anarchist Suggested Essays 53

Accidental Death of an Anarchist Quizzes 56
Quiz 1 Answer Key 60

Accidental Death of an Anarchist Quizzes 62
Quiz 2 Answer Key 67

Accidental Death of an Anarchist Quizzes 69
Quiz 3 Answer Key 73

Accidental Death of an Anarchist Quizzes 75
Quiz 4 Answer Key 79

Accidental Death of an Anarchist Bibliography 81

Essay Accidental Death of an Anarchist as a Play of Social and Political Comment 82

Biography of Dario Fo (1926–)

Dario Fo was born on March 24, 1926, in San Giano, Lombardy, Italy, a small fishing village near the border of Switzerland. He was the oldest of three children born to his peasant mother and railway worker father. Fo grew up listening to local storytellers in San Giano and then in Porto Valtraglia, where his family moved when he was 10. He credits both them and his parents with inspiring his own inventiveness and nurturing his imagination.

Fo came of age during World War II. In 1944, Mussolini took control of Fo's home village; Fo joined the army but deserted soon afterwards. His family was staunchly anti-fascist, helping Jews and Allied prisoners of war escape into neutral Switzerland.

Before and after the war, Fo attended school in Milan. He studied both art and architecture; while he later withdrew from the architecture program, he acquired the skills with which to design his own sets. Fo enjoyed the intellectual life of the city and his growing acquaintance with actors, artists, and writers. Particularly influential were Franco Parenti, an actor with whom he established his first theater company, and Franca Rame, an actress and playwright whom he married in 1954.

Fo's first play was *A Poke in the Eye* (1953), staged with the company he established with Parenti. The drama established Fo as a political playwright, presenting Marxist ideas in a satirical way. His next play, *Madhouse for the Sane* (1954), so enraged government officials that they sent state inspectors to each performance to ensure that he did not violate any libel laws.

After a brief stint writing films in Rome, Fo returned to Milan and to the theater, forming the Compagnia Dario Fo-Franca Rame with his wife. His plays were still satirical, although less explicitly political, and the two performed primarily for bourgeois audiences. In 1962 the couple was invited to perform on the television programme *Canzonissima*, a variety show. The show was immensely popular, but the couple's hard-hitting satire of institutions and individuals led to death threats. When the programme's director refused to allow Fo to perform a sketch on accidents at work during a workers' strike, he and Rame walked out.

In 1968, the couple became disillusioned by what they saw as their role as entertainers for the bourgeoisie. They decided to disband their former company in order to establish a theater cooperative, the Nuovo Scena, backed by the Italian Communist party. Wanting to reach the working class, they performed at nontraditional venues such as workers' clubs, factories, and even football stadiums. Their plays all had a political motive, growing increasingly radical. In 1969 Fo staged arguably his most popular and controversial play, *Mistero buffo,* in which he indicts landowners, the government, and the Catholic Church as oppressors of the people. Eventually the company provoked even the Communist party, which withdrew support due to a play highlighting the party's antirevolutionary policies and its subsequent seduction by capitalism.

In 1970 the couple formed a new cooperative, La Comune, which produced *Accidental Death of an Anarchist*. The play was a huge success, with the troupe performing in, among other places, a sports stadium for over 600 people. Within several years, however, the couple became the target of police brutality and corruption themselves, likely due to their part in exposing the Pinelli scandal. Fo was arrested in Sardinia for supposedly failing to allow police to enter the theater in which he was rehearsing, and his wife was kidnapped and raped by terrorists apparently acting in concert with Italy's main police force.

Fo was not allowed to perform in the United States until 1986, when he and Rame were finally granted visas. They had been denied earlier entry due to their involvement in Red Aid, a group supporting imprisoned left-wing militants and their families.

In 1997, Fo was awarded the Nobel Prize for Literature. The author of over 40 plays, he is considered to be the most widely performed playwright alive today.

Accidental Death of an Anarchist Summary

The first scene of *Accidental Death of an Anarchist* introduces the Maniac, a certified madman with an "acting mania." Bertozzo, a police officer, interviews the Maniac about his latest charge of impersonating a psychiatrist. The Maniac denies any wrongdoing, revealing his quick wit in his responses. When Bertozzo leaves, the Maniac reenters the empty room and looks through Bertozzo's files. The Inspector from the fourth floor calls, looking for Bertozzo; we can infer that a judge is coming to the station to reopen the inquiry about the death of the anarchist. The Maniac pretends Bertozzo is in the room making rude comments about the Inspector and his situation, prompting the Inspector to later punch Bertozzo in the face. Meanwhile, the Maniac decides to impersonate the judge and conduct the inquiry himself.

In the second scene, the Maniac interviews the Inspector and the Superintendent, asking them to recreate what happened the night of the anarchist's death. They told the anarchist they had proof he had planted bombs at the railway station, that his comrade had confessed to planting a bomb at the bank, and that the anarchist's alibi had collapsed. None of these things were actually true. To demonstrate the effects of such "psychological warfare," the Maniac tells the policemen that there is evidence that they were both negligent and that their careers are ruined. He encourages them to jump out the window, as the anarchist had supposedly done, and they both later admit that they seriously considered doing so.

The Maniac admits his deception and offers to help the policemen make their story more coherent. In their second version of events, the anarchist didn't jump until four hours after the interrogation, allowing the men to claim their lies could not have been what caused the anarchist to commit suicide. The Maniac invents details that support this story: the Superintendent put a hand on the anarchist's shoulder, the Inspector pat him on the cheek and told him not to lose heart, and they all sang a song. The policemen object to the fictions, but the Maniac argues that the public would love such a story and they agree to play along.

At the beginning of Act Two, the Maniac says they need to determine what could have happened between 8pm and midnight to cause the anarchist to jump out the window. Instead, however, he points out a number of inconsistencies in the policemen's testimony: the window was open, yet it was midnight in December when the temperature was below zero; the anarchist would have had trouble reaching the window without a running start or a leg-up; and if the constable had really tried to stop him and held onto a shoe, as he said, then the anarchist must have either had three feet or been wearing two shoes on one foot, since witnesses reported he had both shoes on when he landed on the pavement.

The Journalist arrives and the Maniac says he will take on the disguise of the Captain from Forensics to prevent the Journalist from learning that the inquiry has been reopened. His costume includes an eyepatch, a glass eye, and a wooden hand and leg. The journalist brings up additional incriminating evidence against the police. Why did the previous inquiry omit the report on the trajectory taken by the anarchist's body, which would have established whether or not he was alive when he went through the window? Why was an ambulance called for five minutes before the "jump"? Why, too, were there bruises on the back of the dead man's neck? The Maniac explains that there has been a version of events floating around that says that a few minutes before midnight, one of the interrogators lost control of himself and gave the anarchist a whack on the neck. The whack half paralyzed the anarchist, so they called an ambulance. In the meantime, they opened the window and two policemen leaned the anarchist out, hoping the cold air would revive him. However, they accidentally dropped him, each man thinking the other was holding on. The Journalist says the story would explain a lot, including the reason the prosecutor stated the death should be classified as an "accidental death" rather than a suicide. She and the Maniac also discuss the "unreliability" of the witnesses who confirmed the anarchist's alibi.

The play gears up for its climax with the reappearance of Bertozzo, who has brought a copy of the bomb that exploded in the bank. Bertozzo is acquainted with the real Forensics Captain and knows that the Maniac is an imposter. Eventually, he realizes that he is the madman he had been interviewing at the start of the play. The other policemen, thinking Bertozzo will reveal that the Maniac is a judge, kick him and engage in other slapstick humor to try to keep him silent. Bertozzo, meanwhile, tries to dismantle the Maniac's disguise, revealing that there is no reason for the eyepatch or the false leg.

During this time the Journalist continues her questioning, and it comes out that the bomb was very complex - likely the work of the military. She points out that two of the ten members of the anarchist group were spies and asks how the group could have pulled off such an operation while being kept under close scrutiny. The Maniac agrees that the police would have been better off pursuing fascist or paramilitary organizations rather than ragtag anarchist groups. He tells her his beliefs about scandals - they make the public think that the authorities are doing something, but in reality, nothing changes.

The pace quickens as the Maniac switches his disguise to that of Bishop. Bertozzo tries more frantically to reveal the Maniac's identity, and the Inspector and the Superintendent try more frantically to prevent him. Finally, Bertozzo whips out a gun and threatens to shoot. He has the constable handcuff the others to a horizontal bar and orders the Maniac to confess who he really is. The Maniac shares his files and the others are outraged. He grabs the bomb and tells Bertozzo to drop the gun or he will press the detonator and kill them all. When Bertozzo complies, the Maniac reveals a tape recording of their conversations, which he plans to copy and distribute to political entities and the media.

Suddenly the lights go out and the bomb goes off in the courtyard below. When the lights come back on, the Maniac is gone; we can infer he has jumped out the window and fallen to his death. Since neither the journalist nor the handcuffed policemen had anything to do with the Maniac jumping, the Journalist says she may have to rethink her position about the anarchist's jump. She leaves and the policemen take keys out of their pockets and unlock their handcuffs.

There is a knock on the door and the actor who played the Maniac enters. The policemen surround him, thinking he is the Maniac. However, it turns out he is the actual High Court Judge, there to reopen the inquiry into the death of the anarchist.

Note - this ending appears in Simon Nye's translation. Other adaptations feature different endings, including one where the Journalist must decide between saving the evidence or the handcuffed police officers before the bomb detonates. Please see the section on Challenges of Translation for more information.

Accidental Death of an Anarchist Background

Accidental Death of an Anarchist is a form of political theater, written in response to the death of Giuseppi (Pino) Pinelli, an anarchist who died while in police custody for questioning about a bombing in which he played no part. Some of Fo's regular playgoers requested that he write the play to provide counter-information to the misinformation being propagated about the event by the media. He researched the case thoroughly, drawing from two official inquiries as well as facts shared by friendly journalists and lawyers. His aim was to present this counter-information in a way that would be accessible to all.

The event took place in Milan, Italy, in December 1969, at the end of a tumultuous decade. The two main political parties in Italy at the time were the Christian Democrats and the Italian Communists, with underground forces conspiring to keep the Communists out of government, or to introduce a non-democratic system (possibly fascist or totalitarian). Two failed attempts at a *coup d'etat* in 1964 and 1970 added to the sense of unease among the populace. Activists reacted by demanding new politics and advocating for revolution, with students ready to join forces with striking trade unionists. Neo-fascists, meanwhile, began carrying out terrorist attacks blamed on left-wing groups, with the aim of creating a climate of fear in which the public would support a powerful totalitarian regime in order to stop the killing. The "attack on the twenty-fifth" (24) mentioned by the Superintendent in the play refers to two bombings on April 25, 1969 at the Milan Exhibition Center and the railway station, both blamed on left-wing organizations. By blaming the left, this "strategy of tension" was also designed to halt the growth of strength of the working class.

On December 12, 1969, a bomb went off in the Banca dell'Agricoltura in Piazza Fontana, located in the center of Milan. 16 people were killed and another 90 were injured. An hour earlier, a bag of explosives had been found at a different bank in Milan, but it did not detonate; the police blew it up rather than disarming it, thus destroying a key piece of evidence. Nobody knows the full truth of what happened that day, but newspapers reported that anarchist groups were responsible. Giuseppe (Pino) Pinelli was one of the first anarchists to be taken in for questioning. He was detained for three days before "falling" out of a fourth-floor window to his death around midnight on December 15. Another anarchist, ballet dancer Pietro Valpreda, was put in jail for three years for his supposed complicity. Neither Pinelli nor Valpreda were actually involved in the attacks, nor, as far as we know, were any members of anarchist groups.

Inspector Luigi Calabresi was in charge of Pinelli's interrogation. Calabresi, whom many suspected of being sympathetic to the fascists, had blamed the Piazza Fontana bombings on "left-wing extremists" and was unlikely to have been impartial to Pinelli. There were five additional officers in Calabresi's office when Pinelli died, as well as a group of journalists in the courtyard below. An autopsy revealed that Pinelli had bruises on his neck. There were massive inconsistencies between the various reports of what happened that night, a fact Fo capitalizes on throughout the play.

A leftist newspaper called the *Lotta Continua* blamed Calabresi for Pinelli's death, coining or at least popularizing his nickname, "Officer Window-Straddler." Calabresi sued the *Lotta Continua* and its editor, Pio Baldelli, for criminal libel. The case was still ongoing two months later when *Accidental Death of an Anarchist* initially premiered on December 10, 1970, one year after Pinelli's death. The script was adapted for each performance to take into account new developments. The trial was contentious, centering more on the death of Pinelli than Baldelli's libel. At one point Calabresi's lawyer challenged the judge, who was removed from the case.

On May 17, 1972, three days after his bodyguard was declared unnecessary, Calabresi was murdered. Nobody was arrested at the time, but in 1988 a man named Leonardo Marino claimed he had driven Calabresi's killers and named the four supposedly guilty men. All had been members of the *Lotta Continua* in the 1970s. Fo has continued to be interested in the case and wrote *Free Marino! Marino is Innocent!* in 1998 to satirize Marino's evidence.

Accidental Death of an Anarchist has been performed in over 40 countries, including fascist Chile and apartheid South Africa. It is Fo's best-known play and his second most popular play in Italy (after *Mistero Buffo*). While some adaptations have mutated into whimsical farce, Fo intended the play to be intensely political, as it was during its initial run in Italy. The first performance took place just a few hours after a demonstration to commemorate the one-year anniversary of the Piazza Fontana bombing. A student was killed by tear gas fired by police, and the next day 700 participants convened to discuss the death. The day after that, 3,000 people met to vote on how to commemorate the first anniversary of Pinelli's death. They ended up bringing the city center to a halt with pickets, marches, and demonstrations.

Fo did not advertise his play, yet even so, it was so popular - and so timely - that 500 people had to be turned away one night. Fo often performed outside of conventional theaters, such as in public squares or occupied factories, wanting to bring his message to the common people. There was a "third act" in each performance, a debate between the actors and the audience on the issues raised, with the intention of empowering the audience to think critically and hopefully take action. Fo would also typically begin the evening by talking about current events and finishing with a discussion of the historical context. He rewrote the play many times during rehearsals and also made alterations based on public reaction or in response to ongoing events.

It has been difficult to maintain this same intensity of political activism in translation, where the play is stripped of the introduction and the third act, and where audiences are less familiar with the events upon which the play is based. However, Fo has given translators and directors the freedom to adapt the play as they see fit, substituting appropriate cultural and political references and changing the setting. While at times directors have taken this freedom too far in favor of comic effect, Fo's openness to adaptation has helped his message reach audiences around the world, of whom all can relate to corruption found within state institutions.

Accidental Death of an Anarchist Characters

Bertozzo

Bertozzo is the amalgam of several real-life police officers. In Italy, jokes about the *carabinieri*, one of the three police forces, are common; Bertozzo fits the stereotype that is typically the target of these jokes.

We meet Bertozzo at the beginning of the play as he interviews the Maniac regarding his latest impersonation. His lines are humorless and serve as a means for the Maniac to display his own wit. He is absent for the majority of the "inquiry" the Maniac conducts with the Inspector and the Superintendent but returns as the play approaches its climax, bringing in a replica of a bomb destroyed by the police. He recognizes the Maniac and tries to reveal his true identity to the others, but the Superintendent and the Inspector, thinking Bertozzo will admit that the Maniac is a judge to the Journalist, do whatever they can to silence him.

Throughout the play, Bertozzo is the butt of jokes and recipient of mocking laughter and physical abuse. This contributes to the play's slapstick humor, while reminding the audience of the abuse the anarchist likely endured during his interrogation.

The Maniac

The Maniac is the pivotal character in the play. While he has no counterpart in real life, he speaks the majority of the lines and was played by Fo himself in the original staging. It is through the Maniac that Fo satirizes the police, reveals the inconsistencies in their stories, demonstrates the questionable nature of their interrogation techniques, and presents counter-information to what was being presented about the case in the press.

The Maniac has been diagnosed with an "acting mania" and has been charged twelve times for impersonation, most recently while pretending to be a psychiatrist. He uses his talents to investigate what really happened the night of the anarchist's death, adopting the persona first of a judge reopening the inquiry, then a forensics expert, and finally a bishop. Through the Maniac, Fo insinuates that police spies commonly impersonated members of political groups. The Maniac's constantly shifting persona and hyperactive nature may also contribute to the "alienation effect," preventing audience members to become so absorbed in the play that they fail to think critically about its meaning.

The character of the Maniac has its roots in the Italian theatre tradition of *commedia dell'arte*, popular from the mid-16th to the mid-18th centuries. In *commedia dell'arte*, the actors were at the heart of the playmaking process, improvising lines rather than blindly following a script. Plots consisted primarily of stock characters rather than individuals, and actors usually wore masks. The most celebrated character was the Harlequin, or trickster, most commonly seen with a long, hooked nose, a half-mask over his eyes and mouth, and a multicolored costume. Fo's updated version of the Harlequin is devious, irreverent, and a free spirit. He contradicts convention and owes loyalty to none. As a trickster, the Maniac deceives the policemen by interrogating and lying to them, just as they had done to the anarchist. Afterwards he leads them to believe he is on their side, only to later agree with the Journalist in her insinuations of their culpability. At times he plays the role of a clown, convincing the policemen to join him in a rousing song or accidentally swallowing his glass eye. While the Maniac is certifiably insane, the character exposes the true madness of this tumultuous time in Italy's history.

Constables

The constables are foolish bystanders, reminiscent of the bumbling, incompetent policemen of detective stories. They follow orders immediately and agree with whatever anyone says. By depicting the constables as such simple- and single-minded people, Fo pokes fun at the hierarchy of the police bureaucracy.

Though there were four constables in the office at the time of Pinelli's death, there is no direct link to any of the real-life constables to the characters in the play.

Inspector

The Inspector is based closely on commissario Luigi Calabresi, who was commonly believed by leftist organizations to have been directly involved with the death of the anarchist Pino Pinelli. He told the media that the far left was responsible for the Piazza Fontana bombings despite having no proof, led the police raid on the anarchist circle, and invited Pinelli to come to the police station. The *Lotta Continua*, a far left newspaper, gave him the nickname the "Window-Straddler" due to his supposed penchant for having suspects sit on the windowsill during interrogations and taunting them to jump. Calabresi had known ties with both the CIA and the Republican Right in the United States and had become a target of hatred. In his libel suit against the editor of the *Lotta Continua*, the focus of the court case shifted to whether Calabresi had caused the anarchist's death. The case had just begun proceedings when the play originally premiered.

In the play, the Inspector believes that the Maniac is a judge who has come to reopen the inquiry into the death of the anarchist. He tries to prove his innocence, but ends up incriminating himself through the Maniac's clever questioning. Fo satirizes Calabresi mercilessly, using the Maniac to point out the inconsistencies in his story.

He also depicts him as having a temper and lacking a sense of humor, punching Bertozzo in the face when he thinks he has ridiculed him.

Superintendent

The Superintendent is based on Marcello Guida, the head of police in Milan. While he was not present at Pinelli's death, he took part in the cover-up, denying at first any records of the interrogation and later changing his story. He was also involved in the framing of Pietro Valpreda, another anarchist who was wrongly accused of planting bombs and imprisoned for three years. Guida had been a government official under Mussolini and led a prison camp for anti-fascist activists during World War II. In this version of the play, references to his prison camp activities were changed to activities with mercenaries in Bosnia to add a historical context familiar to a contemporary British audience.

Like the Inspector, the Superintendent believes that the Maniac is a judge investigating what happened the night of the anarchist's death. He reacts defensively when he thinks the Maniac is against him, but is happy to go along with whatever the Maniac says if it will get him out of trouble. He and the Inspector have somewhat interchangeable roles, as both were guilty of questionable practices that contributed to the anarchist's death.

Journalist

The Journalist was inspired by Camilla Cederna, a real-life journalist who investigated the case of Pino Pinelli's death. She uncovered police corruption and assisted Fo in his research for the play. Unlike the other comedic characters, the Journalist is a straight role. She is an accurate portrayal of an experienced journalist on a quest to reveal the truth. Through her line of questioning, Fo is able to bring up themes such as police infiltration, the government's strategy of tension, and the role of scandals in suppressing revolution.

Because there is no inherent comedic value to the Journalist's lines, some portrayals of the Journalist have been exaggerated through ridiculous costumes or squeaky voice. However, Fo did not intend for her to be funny, but rather to advance the politics of the play.

Accidental Death of an Anarchist Glossary

all and sundry

everyone

anyroad

anyway

bash

attempt

bog-standard

plain, ordinary, normal

boss-eyed

able to look in two directions at once

cretinous

idiotic

drivel

nonsense

faff

to fuss

fob off

to pass off something false as genuine

give a toss

to care about something

gormless

brainless; lacking in intelligence

hoofer

tap-dancer

mickey-taking

making fun of someone or something

muck someone about

to cause problems or trouble for someone

ponce

an effeminate or ostentatious male; a contemptible person

railway shunter

someone who separates and joins the wagons and carriages on trains

rip the piss

to laugh at the expense of someone else

scuppered

in trouble

slag off

to put someone down; insult

sotto

very quietly; under the breath

stitch up

play someone for a fool; often used when framing someone for a crime

take the piss

to make fun of somebody

tetchy

cranky; easily annoyed

top to tail

two people sleeping with heads at opposite ends of the bed

tosspot

a fool or drunkard

Trappist

a type of monk known for their vow of silence

witter on

to ramble, usually about nothing important, and often drunkenly

Tessa

a tax-exempt special savings account (UK)

ISA

individual savings account

Accidental Death of an Anarchist Themes

Reform versus Revolution

The merit of reform vs. revolution was an ongoing debate in Italy when Fo wrote the play. In the light of the Pinelli scandal, among others, the public weighed the options of how best to address widespread corruption. On the one hand, reformers sought to improve the existing system, whereas revolutionaries aimed to entirely restructure society and institutions. Advocates of the latter tend to think of reform as a mere band-aid, incapable of bringing about real change.

Accidental Death of an Anarchist is a revolutionary play, reflecting Fo's own politics. The Maniac expresses his believe in revolution in his discourse about scandals:

> "People say they want real justice... so we fob them off with a *slightly* less unjust system of justice. Workers howl that they're being flayed like donkeys... so we arrange for the flaying to be a *little* less severe and slash their howling entitlement, but the exploitation goes on. The workforce would rather not have fatal accidents in the factory... so we make it a teeny bit safer and increase compensation payments to widows. They'd like to see class divisions eliminated... so we do our best to bring the classes marginally closer or, preferably, just make it seem that way. They want a revolution... and we give them reforms. We're drowning them in reforms. Or promises of reforms, because let's face it, they're not actually going to get anything" (74-5).

In case his message was not already exceedingly clear, Fo included a note at the end of the script explicitly stating that the police and the judiciary represented a part of the bourgeois state that needed to be overturned.

Fear and Submission

In the late 1960s/early 1970s, Italy experienced a great deal of social unrest. The authorities felt threatened by those on the far left (like Fo) who advocated revolution over reform, as such a radical restructuring of society would eliminate their own power and control. Fascist organizations and members of the police force began committing terrorist acts and blaming them on the far left, hoping that the public would demand a strong crackdown on their enemies. These terrorist acts created a climate of fear, in which people were unlikely to push for major change.

Both the Maniac and the journalist allude to this "strategy of tension." The Journalist brings up the theme of police infiltration into political groups, and the Maniac adds that such infiltrators "also carry out atrocities to give themselves a good excuse for a police crackdown" (70). The Journalist also shares statistics about the number of terrorist attacks carried out by far right organizations:

> "So you'll be unaware that of the 173 bomb attacks to date... 102 have been proved to be the work of fascists? And fascist or parallel organisations were strongly implicated in half of the remaining seventy-one cases" (72).

Nearly all of those attacks, she adds, were made to look like the work of the far left.

Corruption

While the play documents a specific event, it is ultimately an exposition of police corruption in Italy during the 1960s and 1970s, with allusions to government collusion. While nobody will ever know the complete truth about both the anarchist's death and who is responsible for the *Piazza Fontana* bombings, the play brings to light the blatant lies told about the case by the police, pointing out the obvious inconsistencies and omission of key evidence in the official police reports. Through farce and wordplay, Fo is able to satirize the bureaucracy and hypocrisy of the police force. Though the play is comic, Fo is communicating the serious consequences corruption reaps on the public - misinformation, fear, and violence.

Madness

Is the Maniac truly crazy, or is it the world around him that is mad? Does madness mean being separated from reality, or simply seeing the world differently than others? The Maniac behaves in a paradoxical way: he engages in increasingly more elaborate lies and disguises, yet he does so in order to reveal the truth. Might it really be the Inspector and the Superintendent who are mad, accepting even the Maniac's most outrageous lies in order to keep their own culpability hidden? By making the protagonist a maniac who outwits corrupt and volatile authority figures, Fo suggests the institution, and not the man, is the true fount of madness.

Truth and Illusion

One of the play's core messages is that authority figures are more concerned with maintaining an illusion that protects their position of power than they are with uncovering the truth. The Inspector and the Superintendent's attacks on Bertozzo in Act II symbolize the way that the police have undermined the truth in order to preserve their own status. It is ironic that the most outrageous liar - the Maniac - is also the most dedicated to the truth.

Fo uses the Maniac's quick wit to show how language can be manipulated to utterly confuse and disguise the truth. After provoking the Inspector by pretending that Bertozzo has blown him a raspberry, for instance, the Maniac twists his words around to deflect attention away from what really happened:

> INSPECTOR: I bet Bertozzo didn't mention his joke about low-rise police stations in Huddersfield and the raspberries...
>
> SUPERINTENDENT: Raspberries in Huddersfield - what are you wittering on about? ....
>
> MANIAC: ....I now discover from what you were saying that he's allergic to raspberries from the north of England - which, between you and me, are really rather bland, especially compared to free-range raspberries from say, Scotland or Jersey. (20-21)

Through exchanges like this, Fo illustrates how easily the truth can be manipulated.

Layers of Reality

The play suggests that there are many layers to reality. We never learn what definitively happened the night of the anarchist's death, although what likely happened is slowly revealed. For instance, at first it seems the Inspector may have put the anarchist in such a poor mental state that he jumped out the window in desperation, whereas the introduction of additional evidence - bruises on the anarchist's neck, the timing of the ambulance call, the incongruity of having a window open in December - suggest he may not have committed suicide at all, but rather was killed or severely injured in the office with a blow to the neck. Here, the truth is not in the detail, but in the culpability for the man's death. No matter the method, the police killed the anarchist.

The Maniac's disguises also serve as a metaphor for these layers of truth. For instance, the Inspector and the Superintendent think he is really a judge disguised as a forensics officer and later a bishop, yet what they believe to be the truth of his identity ends up being one more layer of disguise. By reminding audience members that they are watching a play, Fo goes one step further: even the Maniac's "true" identity as a madman is a disguise, as he is really just an actor playing a part on the stage. Again, what the madman represents - a foil for the corrupt - is more important than who he *really* is.

Class Oppression

As a member of the far left, Fo saw the flaws in a capitalist society that depends on the stratification of its classes. Fo illustrates this in the Maniac's debate about the three witnesses who confirmed the anarchist's alibi. The judge in the initial inquiry had dismissed the evidence of these witnesses as unreliable, saying, "these people are old, a bit shaky on their feet and basically disabled" (62).

The Maniac points out that the issue is less about age and more about economic class:

> "I admit it, it's true, society is split into classes. And the same obviously goes for witnesses. You've got your first-, second-, third- and fourth-class witnesses. It's not a question of age. You can be frighteningly old and quite breathtakingly out-to-lunch, but if you turn up in court after a bit of work from a crack team of beauticians, a massage, a quick sesh under a sunlamp, in a silk shirt, little scarf, big chauffeur-driven Mercedes - well, then I can't quite see the judge dismissing you as unreliable. I personally would even throw in a bit of gratuitous bowing. 'Super-reliable', that would be my verdict" (64).

Even if lower-class witnesses are less reliable, he points out that it is the inequity of the class system which makes them so: "Can't afford vitamins, protein, organic honey or calcium phosphate to keep your memory sharp? Well, hard lines, I'm the judge and I'm turning you down, you're not up to it, you're a second-class citizen" (63). In this way Fo uses the Maniac to express his own anti-capitalist sentiments.

Accidental Death of an Anarchist Quotes and Analysis

I've worked you out: you really do have this acting mania, so you're acting mad but in fact you're saner than I am.

Bertozzo, p. 7

The Maniac is in fact saner than most; his madness is only a theatrical device. It is ironic that the Maniac is labeled "mad" when he is the character most dedicated to revealing the truth. Even the Journalist admits that her primary motivation is to write a good article, whereas the Maniac has no motive beyond the pursuit of truth. It is also ironic, of course, that in order to uncover what really happened, he has to lie and impersonate others. For this reason it may be the world around him that is truly mad.

No, don't throw me out, Inspector. I love it here with you, among policemen. I feel safe.

Maniac, p. 9

The Maniac's statement is bitterly ironic, since the anarchist was anything but safe among policemen. For audience members unfamiliar with the story, it foreshadows later events in which we learn that the police were almost certainly responsible for the anarchist's death. This wry, dangerous line highlights Fo's sharp comedy, used as a tool against corruption.

SUPERINTENDENT: Those bastards in the government. First they ask you to help - 'Ferment a little subversion, chip in with a bit of repression, go on, spread a sense of gathering disorder...'

INSPECTOR: '...then sit back and wait for calls for a state clampdown!'

Superintendent and Inspector, p. 33

The policemen place the blame for their actions on the government, arguing that they were told to spread a sense of disorder so that the public will demand a firm response and even support a totalitarian state in order to stop the violence. In so doing they voice the "strategy of tension" used by the Italian state at the time of the play's premiere. While Fo satirizes the police and was no friend of Calabresi (the model for the Inspector), with this quote he suggests that despite their shortcomings, the police were in a sense pawns of a larger and more sinister force.

> *...it's not baloney, it's just the usual traps and scams that we in the judiciary use occasionally to remind the police how barbaric and of course illegal those methods are.*
>
> *Maniac, p. 34*

The Inspector and the Superintendent justify their methods of interrogating the anarchist by explaining that they used "a perfectly standard procedure, as practised in every police force, to draw a confession out of the suspect" (24). These methods included engaging in a form of "psychological warfare" in which they invented information that could have caused enough mental anguish to push the anarchist to commit suicide. Rather than merely questioning the morality of such methods, the Maniac demonstrates their effects by using them on the Inspector and the Superintendent. After pointing out the holes in their arguments, he tells them: "Okay, you're probably feeling a little bit depressed right now. So what better time to add that there is damning proof of gross negligence on your part, that you're both dead in the water, and that in an attempt to make the rest of the police look good the Home Office are going to crucify you." (29) He then encourages the Superintendent and the Inspector to jump out the window, which they both admit they seriously considered doing. The Maniac admits to his deception in the quote above, which parallels the Inspector's own justification for using such methods and, in so doing, highlights how corrupt those methods really are.

> *SUPERINTENDENT: I'm delighted to reveal that we have, yes, lots of undercover agents, pretty much everywhere.*
>
> *JOURNALIST: Now I know you're bluffing, Superintendent.*
>
> *SUPERINTENDENT: Not at all. In tonight's audience, for example. We have a few of our people in. Do you want to see?*
>
> *He claps his hands. Voices are heard from various points in the auditorium.*
>
> *VOICES: Superintendent!/ Over here, sir!/ Yessir?*
>
> *The* ***Maniac*** *laughs and turns to the audience.*
>
> *MANIAC: Don't be alarmed, they're drama students. The real undercover ones are trained to sit quietly.*
>
> *Superintendent / Journalist / Maniac, p. 70*

This quote expands on the theme of fear and submission, insinuating that police infiltrators could be anywhere - even at this play. It also demonstrates one of the methods Fo uses to encourage audience members to avoid getting drawn too much into the storyline and instead to think critically about the issues raised.

By having the Superintendent and the Maniac speak directly to the audience, Fo eliminates the invisible "fourth wall" between the actors and the audience. The Maniac's reference to drama students goes one step further, explicitly reminding the audience that they are watching a play.

> *OK. So let's take a look behind that façade. What do we find? Out of the ten members of the [anarchist's] group, two of them were your own people, two informers, or rather, spies and provocateurs. One was a Rome fascist, well-known to everyone except the aforementioned pathetic group of anarchists, and the other was one of your own officers, disguised as an anarchist.*
>
> *Journalist, p. 72*

The Journalist brings up the practice of infiltration, one of the methods through which the police and the government create a climate of fear. In pretending to act for the left, the infiltrators foment uncertainty through acts of violence. This chaos fractures the radicals by muddying the motives and deeds of the political groups. The police hoped to win the public's support for a strong state, trading democratic principles for the security that a totalitarian government could bring.

> *JOURNALIST: You say you don't know anything... So you'll be unaware that of the 173 bomb attacks to date (Reads from document) 102 have been proved to be the work of fascists? And fascist or parallel organisations were strongly implicated in half of the remaining seventy-one cases.*
>
> *SUPERINTENDENT: Those figures may be correct, yes... Any comments, Inspector?*
>
> *INSPECTOR: I'd have to check.*
>
> *JOURNALIST: Good, and while you're at it check how many of those attacks were made to look like the work of far-left groups.*
>
> *INSPECTOR: Well, almost all of them, obviously.*
>
> *Journalist / Superintendent / Inspector, p. 72*

Here the Journalist summarizes the "strategy of tension" alluded to earlier by the Inspector and the Superintendent. By committing terrorist acts and blaming them on the far left, fascists hoped to create public demand for a strong government capable of cracking down on the violence. Fo presented these facts to counter the false information commonly spread by the media.

...the scandal would have served its purpose. People say they want real justice... so we fob them off with a slightly less unjust system of justice. Workers howl that they're being flayed like donkeys... so we arrange for the flaying to be a little less severe and slash their howling entitlement, but the exploitation goes on. The workforce would rather not have fatal accidents in the factory... so we make it a teeny bit safer and increase compensation payments to widows. They'd like to see class divisions eliminated... so we do our best to bring the classes marginally closer or, preferably, just make it seem that way.

They want a revolution... and we give them reforms. We're drowning them in reforms. Or promises of reforms, because let's face it, they're not actually going to get anything.

Maniac, pp. 74-5

This quote reflects Fo's own views on revolution versus reform, a hotly debated topic at the time the play was written. Through the Maniac, Fo argues that reform does very little besides calming the populace down and keeping them under control. Scandals, he says, encourage people to clamor for change, but the small changes that do occur do more to increase the standing of those in power than to actually improve the situation. Fo believed that revolution, and with it a complete overthrow of existing institutions, is the way to create real positive change.

Tensions massaged away through the miracle of catharsis, and you journalists are the over-indulged chief masseuses.

Maniac, p. 80

Fo avoided catharsis, in which spectators purge themselves of emotions such as anger or fear through the act of watching a play and letting their emotions flow through them. Here, he implies that people experience catharsis when reading the news as well. News of scandals rile them up, but then the tensions fade as their negative emotions pass. Fo's aim was the opposite of catharsis; he wanted people to engage in debate, challenge ideas, and consider new points of view.

They've never tried to cover up these scandals. Which is great! So the public can really vent their outrage and disgust: 'What is this government thinking of!?' 'Arsehole generals!' 'Murderers!' So they get cross, then possibly even angry, but then the bubble bursts. It's like a burp. Then the meal is over.

Maniac, p. 81

This quote expands on Fo's ideas of reform versus revolution and the detriments of catharsis. Scandals let people express their anger, but once expressed, this anger dissipates. Paradoxically, exposing scandals thus serves to maintain the status quo, possibly bringing about a few minor reforms that satisfy the public's desire for a government response while avoiding true revolutionary change.

Accidental Death of an Anarchist Study Guide: Act One, Scene One Summary and Analysis

Summary

The scene opens in a room on the third floor of police headquarters. The Maniac's face appears at the window. He opens the window and climbs inside with a large bag.

Inspector Bertozzo and a Constable enter through the door. Bertozzo checks the Maniac's file and notes he has a charge against him for impersonation, his twelfth. He is mad, diagnosed with "acting mania". Most recently he played a psychiatrist and charged two hundred pounds to diagnose a boy with schizophrenia, a charge he justifies by claiming the boy's family wouldn't have taken him seriously otherwise. He also denies that his business card constitutes fraud due to the placement of commas and periods.

The Maniac continues his quick-witted banter, quoting articles from the penal code, and Bertozzo expresses surprise that the Maniac has yet to impersonate a judge. The Maniac responds that he would love to: it's the best job in the world because, unlike most jobs where people are less valued as they get older, a judge is promoted each passing year. Bertozzo offers to let the Maniac go as soon as he takes down his statement, but the Maniac says he would rather stay and, if he is not allowed to do so, he'll throw himself out the window. Bertozzo has the Constable lock the window and pushes the Maniac out the door. Bertozzo and the Constable leave for a meeting.

The Maniac reenters and, seeing the office empty, rifles through arrest sheets he sees on the desk. He destroys some and keeps others, then opens a cupboard full of files. One, labeled 'Judge's Decision To Terminate Inquiry Into Death At Police Headquarters', catches his eye. As he begins to read, the phone rings and the Maniac answers. The caller is the Inspector from the fourth floor. From the Maniac's side of the conversation we can infer that the Inspector has heard a judge is coming to the station to reopen the investigation about the death of an anarchist who fell out of a fourth-story window while under police custody. The Maniac pretends that Bertozzo is in the room and is making rude comments about the Inspector and his situation, including blowing him a raspberry. Angrily, the inspector responds that the next time he sees Bertozzo, he will punch him in the face.

When the Maniac hangs up, he realizes he can impersonate the aforementioned judge and practices his disguise, borrowing a coat and hat from the rack. Bertozzo returns and the Maniac warns him that someone is looking for him to punch him in the face. The Maniac leaves and Bertozzo notices his coat and hat are missing. He sends the Constable after the Maniac to get them, but the Constable is detained by the

Inspector from the fourth floor who has just arrived. The scene ends with an arm stretched out from the doorway punching Bertozzo in the face. He collapses and the Maniac reappears, shouting, "I told you to duck!"

Analysis

Accidental Death of an Anarchist dramatizes (through farce) the real-life case of the 1969 death of Italian anarchist Giuseppe "Pino" Pinelli, who died in police custody after being blamed for a terrorist attack. The play first premiered in Italy less than a year after Pinelli's death, written by outspoken leftist Dario Fo in an effort to expose corruption and inspire activism. The play has since been performed in over 40 countries, each version adapted to correspond to the cultural and political context in which it is performed, maintaining Fo's intention of drama as a tool to stoke critical thought. Even the original play was rewritten many times during rehearsals, and Fo sometimes altered the script during performances based on the public's reaction or in response to current events. The language of the play is idiomatic, appealing to the nonelite, as Fo encouraged translators to use local slang in place of his own. He encouraged translators to change cultural references to maintain relevance. Thus, this translation by Simon Nye is full of British slang (e.g., tosspot, bird-witted ponce, piss-taking) and contains allusions a British audience would understand.

The Maniac is the main character of the play. He is presented as a quick-witted trickster, a character familiar in comic tradition. Fo was inspired by the *commedia dell'arte* archetype the Harlequin, a member of the underclass who comically thwarts a higher-up by outwitting them. Here, the Maniac acts as a foil for the police, asserting the worthiness of the common people despite the disdain they are shown by the authorities. Although the Maniac is said to be mad, the play will reveal that he is actually more sensible than anyone else.

The opening interchange between the Maniac and Bertozzo sets the mood of the play as a knockabout farce, a type of comedy that entertains through highly exaggerated and improbable situations, the deliberate use of absurdity, and physical humor. The Maniac's twisting of language and grammar when discussing his business card introduces the way that language can be used as a tool of deception, as the political elite and state-sponsored media have done to promote their own cause.

One of Fo's purposes is to educate his audience, and much of the play shares what probably happened when Pinelli was detained. The blame placed on the anarchist was specious at best, and the prevailing theory was that Pinelli fell or was thrown out of the window. Accidental or not, the police were culpable for Pinelli's death. The Maniac's darkly comic jokes repeatedly reference the circumstances of the anarchist's death. He says ironically, "No, don't throw me out, Inspector. I love it here with you, among policemen. I feel safe" (9). The Maniac continues, making his intention more obvious: "Inspector, let me stay, or I'll throw myself out of the window" (10).

The scene also contains several allusions to real people and events. The Maniac finds a file entitled "Judge's Decision to Terminate Inquiry Into Death At Police Headquarters" (11); there was such an inquiry carried out by a judge who concluded that the death had been an accident. The Maniac refers to the Inspector on the phone as Inspector Throws-Anarchists-Out-the-Windows, letting the audience know that this character is meant to represent Luigi Calabresi; there was a rumor that he would invite suspects to sit on his window ledge and taunt them to jump. As noted above, the Maniac also asks the Inspector if his boss used to run a mercenary outfit in Bosnia; in the original version of the play, this was a reference to a prison camp for anti-fascists. Marcello Guida, chief of police during the Pinelli incident - and the model for the Superintendent - ran a prison camp in southern Italy. Finally, there is an allusion to dancer Pietro Valpredo, the other anarchist arrested while Pinelli was in custody.

Devices meant to engage the audience also occur in Scene One. The Maniac reflects on how much he would like to be a judge, foreshadowing his later impersonation. As he tries on different personas, he engages directly with the audience, telling them, "At last, my chance to take my place among the Great and the Good. I feel rather emotional actually." (13) Addressing the audience breaks the illusion of the "fourth wall," the imaginary barrier between audience and actors that allows for suspension of disbelief. As a political playwright, Fo deliberately utilized such techniques to prevent audience members from losing themselves in the story, believing that it was necessary for them to maintain some distance in order to think critically about the issues raised by the play. Another way to achieve this distance (what playwright Bertolt Brecht termed the "alienation effect") is to include self-reflexive strategies, in which the play refers to itself as a play. The Maniac does so when he comments on himself as an actor:

> "I've been admitted sixteen times with what's called 'acting mania'. It's more of a hobby, really - playing other people. I'll do anybody! But the thing is I'm a huge fan of the Theatre of Life, so my fellow actors have to be real people... who don't know they're acting. Which is just as well because I'm a bit short of funds, so I can't pay them" (4).

The last few pages of Scene One are full of bawdy and slapstick humor. The Maniac blows a raspberry at the Inspector, which makes a farting sound; in response, the Inspector punches Bertozzo in the face and he falls flat on the ground. Such humor is appropriate for a populist play, since humor is universal. Fo believed that laughter allows people to hold on to their anger, whereas crying frees them from pain. Wanting his audience to leave the theater transformed and ready for action, he used humor to engage viewers' emotions without allowing them to dissipate.

Accidental Death of an Anarchist Study Guide: Act One, Scene Two Summary and Analysis

Summary

Scene Two takes place in a different room in the police station. There is a large, open window in front of which the Maniac stands. The Inspector enters, massaging his hand, and asks a Constable what the Maniac wants. The Maniac quizzes him comically about his hand, then asks to close the window, which the Inspector dryly refuses to allow.

The Maniac introduces himself as Lord Justice Malcolm, first counsel to the High Court, here to reexamine the facts surrounding the death of the anarchist. He has come early, he explains, to catch the Inspector and his boss off guard. The Inspector is visibly nervous and sends the Constable to fetch the Superintendent. He picks up the phone to call Bertozzo, but the Maniac says that isn't necessary as he has all the paperwork already.

The Superintendent bursts in and chastises the Inspector for giving him orders and for punching Bertozzo. He sees the Maniac and the two exchange humorous words about the Inspector. Once the Superintendent learns who the Maniac supposedly is, the Maniac introduces the case. The anarchist, he reminds them, had been seized by a "raptus" (a type of suicidal anguish) that prompted him to throw himself out the window. He then asks the policemen to reconstruct what happened.

The Superintendent explains how on the night of the anarchist's death, he told the anarchist that they had proof he planted bombs at the railway station. In truth, they had none; they merely assumed he was guilty as he was the only anarchist railwayman in town. The Maniac notes that the anarchist had committed suicide in part out of fear of losing his job, and so infers that the Superintendent must have frightened him about that as well. The Inspector interjects that he told the anarchist his dancer comrade had confessed to planting a bomb at the bank, and that the anarchist took the news badly. The Inspector also told him that his alibi - that he had been playing cards all afternoon - had collapsed. The Maniac notes that the Superintendent later stated there was no proof that implicated the anarchist, and the Superintendent admits they made a mistake. He claims it was necessary to use a little "psychological warfare" in order to do their jobs.

The Maniac is unsympathetic, pointing out that the Superintendent lied not only to the suspect but also to the media. He reveals that there is damning evidence that both the Inspector and the Superintendent were negligent and that their careers are ruined.

Naturally, the two are visibly upset. The Maniac encourages them to jump out the window, since all hope is gone. He even pushes them to the ledge by force.

The Constable reenters and the three other men return to the floor. The Superintendent and the Inspector admit that they had both seriously considered throwing themselves out the window. They blame the government, who has asked them to foment a sense of disorder. The Maniac, however, suddenly admits that he made everything up and that the Ministry is happy with the two policemen. However, he says their panic has proven that they drove the anarchist to throw himself out the window. The Inspector argues that they weren't even present when the anarchist jumped, which the constable confirms. The Superintendent, however, reminds them all that they should be talking about the second version of the facts they had presented rather than the first. In that version, the policemen lied about their evidence at 8pm, but the anarchist didn't jump until four hours later, at midnight. Therefore, it couldn't have been their misinformation that prompted the suicide, since so much time had passed.

The Maniac now appears to be on the policemen's side. He says they must prove that by the end of those four hours the anarchist had completely recovered from the mental anguish he suffered as a result of the policemen's lies. They decide that the anarchist and the dancer were no longer friends anyway and so the anarchist was not so upset about the dancer having planted a bomb, although the Maniac points out that the first version of the report noted how depressed he was. The Maniac decides that something must have helped the anarchist to change his mood. He comes up with a story: the policemen were saddened by the anarchist's anguish, so the Superintendent put a hand on the anarchist's shoulder and the Inspector pat him on the cheek. The Inspector then told the anarchist not to lose heart - anarchy would never die - and they all sang a song. The policemen object to the fictions, but the Maniac argues that the public would love such a story. The scene ends as they all sing an anarchist protest song.

Analysis

This scene is comprised both of slapstick humor and serious interludes, in which anger overcomes laughter. Fo deliberately intersperses such moods in an attempt to rouse his audience to action. The play was never intended to be pure comedy, but rather an emotionally effective tool to educate the audience and leave them with enough unsettled feelings to inspire them to take action.

The scene reveals the central conflict of the play: the Maniac wishes to reveal the truth, while the Inspector and the Superintendent seek to conceal it and exonerate themselves. The characters' zeal to achieve these opposing goals leads to increasingly ridiculous and comical dialogue.

As the scene begins the Inspector is rubbing his hand, having just punched Bertozzo in the face. The Maniac asks, "What's wrong with your hand?... If it's nothing, why are you rubbing it? What is it, an affectation? Some kind of nervous tic?" (17) In their coverage of the Pinelli case, Italian newspapers noted the compulsive movements and other nervous habits of Calabresi, the real-life inspector who interrogated the anarchist; the reference thus reconfirms that the Inspector represents Calabresi. As they talk, the Maniac refers several times to the open window, never letting attention stray too far from the issue at hand.

As the Maniac plays the part of judge, two themes emerge: first, that the police are using informants to create a climate of fear; and second, that the police cannot be trusted to tell the truth. "We have informants as well, you know," the Maniac says, explaining that he has come early to catch the policemen off guard. We also see how quickly the Inspector changes his story when the Maniac asks him if his presence bothers him. At first he responds "Not in the slightest," but when the Maniac draws attention to his twitching neck - supposedly a nervous tic of a liar - the Inspector changes his answer to "Or rather... yes it does. A lot." (19)

The Maniac again demonstrates the way in which language can be manipulated to disguise the truth. When the Superintendent reprimands the Inspector for punching Bertozzo, the Inspector tries to defend himself by explaining that Bertozzo had blown him several raspberries. The Maniac quick-wittedly turns his words around: "Yes, I'd already marked him out as somewhat tetchy, and I now discover from what you were saying that he's allergic to raspberries from the north of England - which, between you and me, are really rather bland, especially compared to free-range raspberries from say, Scotland or Jersey" (21). The Superintendent, now utterly confused, lets the matter slide.

As in Scene One, the translator has modified cultural references to make the play resonate with a British audience. Fo gives his translators freedom to change the text however they wished in order to speak to their own audiences - a reflection both on his sense of populism and the weight he placed on the political aspect of his plays. For example, in the original, the Maniac asks the Superintendent if he used to run an anti-fascist camp in southern Italy - a reference to Marcello Guida, head of police Milan at the time of the Pinelli case. But in this version the Maniac asks if the Superintendent was "connected with the supply of freelance troops to the Balkans" in the early 1990s. This is a reference to the 1992-1995 Bosnian war, a territorial conflict between political and cultural factions in Bosnia and Herzegovena. Incidents of "ethnic cleansing", genocidal massacres of one group by another - e.g. the slaughter of 8,000 Muslim Bosniaks by the Orthodox Serbians in the 1995 Srebrenica massacre - became endemic to this conflict. The nature of this allusion carries the same weight as Fo's original reference.

Fo does not alter the tone when the Maniac brings up the case around which the play revolves, maintaining instead a flippant, comic mood appropriate to farce. He does, however, draw upon many real-life facts from the case. The Maniac's use of the term "early stages" refers to the fact that there were several versions of what happened the night of the anarchist's death. The Maniac also explains the Inspector's assertion that the anarchist was "seized by a raptus" (23) and threw himself out the window to his death by quoting an imaginary authority figure (Bandieu), thereby ridiculing the real-life judge's report which was full of references to medical and legal experts on suicide.

Scene Two contains an element of self-reflexiveness as the Maniac has the Superintendent and the Inspector reconstruct the events of the night of the anarchist's death, in essence having them create a play within a play. Such a device extends the "alienation effect" and reminds the audience that they are watching a play, allowing them to maintain the distance necessary to think critically about the issues raised.

The scene also points out some of the controversial methods used by the police in times of corruption. For instance, the Superintendent's "proof" that he was an anarchist railwayman is that of coincidence, not evidence. The Maniac uses irony to poke holes in this argument:

> "Absolutely, it's blindingly obvious. So if the bombs must have been put on the train by a railway worker, we can deduce that the bombs that went off at the Law Courts were planted by a judge, that the Memorial to the Unknown Soldier was bombed by a soldier, and the bomb at the Bank of Agriculture was the work of either a banker or a cow" (25).

The Superintendent tries to justify his actions, explaining, "Our job is to interrogate suspects...[a]nd in order to make them talk, from time to time we need to use stratagems, little traps and a certain amount of psychological warfare". (28) Such methods, of course, can often have tragic results. The Maniac turns the tables on the police. He tells them: "...there is damning proof of gross negligence on your part," and that "the Home Office are going to crucify you" (29). He then encourages them to jump out the window since their case is so hopeless. Later he admits he made everything up, just as the Superintendent and the Inspector had done in an attempt to extract a confession from the anarchist. Yet both men also admitted they seriously considered throwing themselves out the window, vividly illustrating the point that the deceptive methods and "psychological warfare" so commonly used by the police could easily have prompted a suspect to commit suicide.

Another emerging theme is government complicity in this deception. The Superintendent and the Inspector both blame the government for the situation the Maniac has led them to believe they are in, summarizing the "strategy of tension" behind its campaign of terror: "Those bastards in the government. First they ask you to help - 'Ferment a little subversion, chip in with a bit of repression, go on, spread a sense of gathering disorder...' '...then sit back and wait for calls for a state clampdown!' So you get stuck in...." (33) The Maniac, too, reiterates this government strategy as he thinks up what the anarchist might have said to his dancer comrade: "'The police and the fascists are using you to create a sense of unrest. Your group's full of paid *agent provocateurs* who can manipulate you as they like. And it's the left who'll end up with egg on its face...'" (37-8).

A staunch socialist, Fo ridicules the hierarchy and trustworthiness of the police department through comic remarks. When the Inspector begins, "So have I got this right - ?" (33), the Superintendent interrupts, asserting his authority: "Of course you haven't. Let me do the talking" (34). The Maniac, too, humorously tells the Inspector, "Who asked you? Please let your superior do the talking. That is *incredibly* rude. Only speak when you're asked a question, is that clear?" (24). Fo also ridicules the several accounts of what happened the night of the anarchist's death, and begins to point out the myriad inconsistencies in their reports. The Maniac refers to the second version of the story as "The Facts, The Remake" (37).

At the end of the scene, the Maniac twists around the officers' words into a new, hilarious version of the facts. He does so by playing on their egos and sense of self-preservation. Earlier in the scene, the Superintendent said his deputy entered the room with the anarchist rather than him, but the Maniac retorted it is unattractive to blame one's subordinates. The Superintendent quickly changes his story and agrees that yes, he accompanied the anarchist. Now, when the Superintendent again says he wasn't in the room with the anarchist, the Maniac responds "No, you have to be there, this is a crucial moment," and he again changes his story: "Okay, I was there." (39) As the conversation progresses, the revisions get more and more ridiculous. The Maniac says he bets the Superintendent couldn't help putting a friendly hand on the anarchist's shoulder, and that the Inspector then gave him a pat on the cheek and said 'Come on, come on, don't lose heart - you wait, anarchy will never die!' (41) In each case, the men object but then agree with the Maniac's story, with encouragement from the Constable. The scene concludes with the policemen singing an anarchist protest song, which the Maniac insists they must say they sang with the anarchist in order to win the public's sympathies. In this way Fo makes the point that stories - even those in the official record - can be very easily invented, and that the truth can be easily twisted by those who know how to manipulate language.

Accidental Death of an Anarchist Study Guide: Act Two, Part 1 Summary and Analysis

Summary

Act Two picks up where Act One left off. The men finish singing, and the Maniac says they have now proven (through his invented story) that the anarchist must have been feeling pretty relaxed. The question is, what happened between this point and midnight to cause him to have his "raptus" and jump out the window? The Superintendent tries to answer, but the Maniac reminds him that he wasn't there - or at least, the easiest way to prove he is innocent is to say he wasn't there.

The Inspector explains that he, four constables, and a sergeant spent that time questioning the anarchist. They did so in a "jokey manner" (44), a term which the Maniac mocks. Most of the jokes were about the anarchist's dancer friend, the Inspector notes, and he agrees with the Maniac that the anarchist must have taken offense and therefore thrown himself out the window. However, the Superintendent reminds them that they had already determined the two anarchists didn't get along anymore. The Maniac infers the anarchist railwayman must have been pretending to be upset to give himself a reason for committing suicide and threw himself out the window in order to destroy the policemen's reputations. The policemen express doubt at the story, and the Maniac agrees it is ridiculous; however, the policemen's version, he says, is even less believable.

The Superintendent asks to close the window, as it is getting cold. The Maniac uses the request to segue into another logical inconsistency in the policemen's story: that the window was wide open at midnight in December, when the temperature was below zero. He also asks who gave the anarchist a leg-up, as it would have been extremely difficult for him to reach the window. The constable notes that he tried to stop the anarchist but only managed to catch hold of his shoe, which came off in his hand. However, witnesses reported that the anarchist was wearing two shoes when he reached the pavement. Did the constable put the shoe back on in flight, or did the anarchist perhaps have three feet? The Maniac proposes a solution: the anarchist was wearing a galosh over one of his shoes, and that is what the constable caught.

The front desk calls to let the Superintendent know that a journalist has come to see him. He wants to refuse, but the Maniac advises him to let her up as she could cause trouble if angered. The Superintendent assumes the Maniac will leave so the Journalist won't find out there is a judge investigating the case. The Maniac says he would never abandon his friends in a time of need and decides to change character, becoming Captain Mark Weeny from Forensic. By the time the Journalist arrives, the

Maniac has adopted a false moustache, a patch over one eye, and a brown glove. He later indicates that the patch covers a glass eye and the glove, an artificial hand.

The Journalist begins her questioning. She asks the Inspector why he is called the Window-Straddler, reading a letter written by another anarchist stating that, during his interrogation, the Inspector had forced him to sit on the windowsill with his legs dangling outside. She continues the inquisition by noting that the previous inquiry did not include the report on the trajectory taken by the anarchists's body, which would have established whether or not he was alive when he went through the window. Furthermore, the inquiry also left out the evidence of a tape recording of the time an ambulance was called, which occurred five minutes before the anarchist supposedly jumped. The Superintendent, Inspector, and Maniac all give ridiculous answers - sometimes they call ambulances just in case something happens and this time they were correct; they were thinking ahead; or perhaps the reporters' or ambulance station's watches were fast or slow. The Inspector gives the Maniac a slap on the back to commend him for his answer, and the Maniac's glass eye pops out.

The Journalist is unconvinced and asks about the bruises on the back of the dead man's neck. The Maniac explains that there has been a version of events floating around that says that a few minutes before midnight, one of the interrogators lost control of himself and gave the anarchist a whack on the neck. The whack half paralyzed the anarchist, so they called an ambulance. In the meantime, they opened the window and two policemen leaned the anarchist out, hoping the cold air would revive him. However, they accidentally dropped him, each man thinking the other was holding on. The Journalist says the story would explain a lot, including the reason the prosecutor stated the death should be classified as an "accidental death" rather than a suicide. As they speak, the Inspector slips on the Maniac's glass eye, and the Constable fetches some water to rinse it off. When he returns, the Maniac takes a drink and accidentally swallows the eye.

The Superintendent and the Inspector are both concerned about the story the Maniac has offered, but the Maniac says he will prove it is unreliable. The Journalist notes that the judge conducting the inquiry similarly dismissed the evidence given by three witnesses as unreliable because the witnesses were elderly and disabled. The Maniac says that yes, ex-workers without the money to purchase supplements or medications to keep their memories sharp are lower-class witnesses, although if an old witness turned up well-dressed in a Mercedes, his testimony would most certainly be accepted. The Maniac comes out from behind the desk, and everyone is surprised to see that he is wearing a wooden leg.

Analysis

The action builds in Act Two as the Maniac points out logical inconsistencies in the police reports that require even more ridiculous fabrications to explain than those he invented in Act One. The farcical elements increase, with characters acting increasingly desperate, and there is an element of mystery as more and more information is revealed.

There is a darkening of tone with the introduction of the Journalist, whose lines are serious and present additional evidence implicating the police. To balance the increasing seriousness of the inquiry, the Maniac's antics become more and more outrageous. He wears a false moustache, a patch over one eye, a brown glove covering a wooden hand, and a fake leg. His glass eye falls out when the Inspector slaps him on the back, and later he swallows the eye when he goes to rinse it off. The dramatic moments caused by the Journalist's assertions are interspersed with moments of knockabout humor, as Fo believed laughter helped the audience to think about topics and would eventually lead them to act.

Much of the Maniac's disguise holds symbolic value. His eye, hand, and leg are all false, as is his identity. The eye may symbolize the way in which people are willing to look at things through false eyes if it suits their purposes, yet the fact that it pops out and is later dirtied suggests that such false ways of seeing things cannot be sustained.

Fo continues to satirize police bureaucracy, and by extension, bureaucratic institutions in general; for instance, the Maniac tells the Constable to shut up because, "only senior officers can swear" (46). He introduces the themes of undercover informants, expanded upon in the second part of the act, and class privilege, as expressed through the unequal treatment of witnesses: "Can't afford vitamins, protein, organic honey or calcium phosphate to keep your memory sharp? Well, hard lines, I'm the judge and I'm turning you down, you're not up to it, you're a second-class citizen" (63).

Fo also continues to draw on facts of the Pinelli case for colorful details in the play. The anarchist dancer really did have a limp, as the officers joked. The details the Maniac gives about the dancer sewing beads onto Liberty lampshades come from the report by Judge Amati, who conducted the first inquiry into the anarchist's death and who implied that these materials could have been used to make bombs. The Constable's assertion that he grabbed on to one of the anarchist's shoes to try to save him was one of the more heroic stories that emerged about the supposed efforts the policemen had taken to keep the anarchist from jumping. The Journalist's line of questioning about the trajectory taken by the body had been the topic of debate in the media in the weeks after the anarchist's death, and the phrase "accidental death" also appeared in Judge Amati's report.

The language, as in Act One, is idiomatic, although the Journalist speaks with more formality than the others. The translator has kept the language colorful through other means as well, such as the alliteration in the Maniac's declaration: "So you're scuppered by your sheer sense of honesty, while this spiteful little anarchist is lying in his grave smirking!" (48) These linguistic fireworks boost the comic elements of the play as it draws to a close, setting the stage for more serious questions.

Accidental Death of an Anarchist Study Guide: Act Two, Part 2 Summary and Analysis

Summary

The play gears up for its climax with the reappearance of Bertozzo, wearing a bandage over one eye. He has come to deliver a metal box containing a copy of the bomb that exploded in the bank. The Maniac introduces himself as Captain Mark Weeny, but Bertozzo is acquainted with the real Weeny and knows the Maniac is lying about his identity. The Superintendent and the Inspector both kick Bertozzo and tell him he doesn't know Weeny; the Maniac kicks him and smacks his head. The three men continue to kick and slap Bertozzo, and each other, trying to get him to understand that the Maniac (whom they believe to be a judge) is only pretending to be Mark Weeny to fool the Journalist.

Upon hearing that Bertozzo is an explosives expert, the Journalist asks him why the policemen blew up a bomb that was found rather than disconnecting it and having forensics test it, as doing so would have given them an additional piece of evidence. The Maniac, in his role as Head of Forensic, explains that the bomb is so complicated it would be easy to hide a second timing device inside of it with a delayed action, and that by the time they dismantled the bomb it could have gone off and killed more people. The Journalist is convinced and the Inspector shakes the Maniac's wooden hand, which comes off.

Bertozzo agrees that the real bomb was very complex - professional and probably military - and the three men, sensing what the Journalist will infer, kick him. The Journalist asks why the policemen went after a disorganized group of anarchists even though the bombs used required professional and probably military expertise. She also points out that at least two of the ten members of the anarchist group were working for the police as informants, with one a known fascist. The Superintendent argues that such spies are essential to their preparedness and says they have undercover agents pretty much everywhere, even in tonight's audience. He claps his hands, and voices call out from various points in the auditorium. The Maniac tells the audience not to be alarmed and that the voices belong to drama students, since the real undercover agents are taught to keep quiet.

The Journalist asks how, if informants were keeping the anarchist group under such close scrutiny, the members would have been able to pull off such a complex bombing operation. The Superintendent says their undercover agent wasn't with the group in the days prior to the bombing and denies that the fascist informer had any connection with the police, claiming ignorance when the Journalist points out he had a parking space at Police Headquarters. The Maniac commends the

Superintendent for his stonewalling, the Superintendent shakes his hand, and the Maniac's wooden hand falls off again; he replaces it with a woman's hand. The Journalist continues, noting that of 173 bomb attacks to date, 102 have been caused by fascists, with half of the remainder likely the work of fascists as well. Nearly all were made to implicate leftist organizations. The Maniac says he supposes the Journalist would argue that the police should have concentrated on pursuing fascist and paramilitary organizations rather than anarchists. The Superintendent expects the Maniac to come up with a brilliant comeback, but instead the Maniac agrees that yes, they could have uncovered a lot of dirt that way.

The Superintendent says the Maniac has gone mad, and Bertozzo realizes the man's true identity. He tries to tell the Superintendent and the Inspector, who think he finally realized the Maniac is really a judge. Bertozzo rips off the Maniac's eyepatch in an attempt to reveal the fraud, but nobody understands.

Meanwhile, the Maniac and the Journalist discuss scandals. The Maniac explains how scandals make the public think that the authorities are doing something, but that in reality, nothing changes. The people want a revolution, but the authorities give them only reforms, or the promise of reforms.

Bertozzo continues his quest to reveal the Maniac's identity, pointing out that his false leg is strapped on at the thigh. The other three policemen drag him off, saying he's wanted on the telephone, and tell him they have to keep the fact that the inquiry has been reopened a secret. Bertozzo is confused. The Superintendent hits him on the knuckles with the phone and tells him to call somebody.

The Maniac, in the meantime, says he has revealed his actual identity to the Journalist: a bishop. Bertozzo expresses his exasperation, and the Inspector wedges a large rubber stamp in Bertozzo's mouth. The Maniac puts on a red skullcap, reveals a crucifix under his jacket, and dons a large ring with a purple stone. Everyone kisses the ring except Bertozzo, who refuses. The Inspector and the constable stick plaster on his mouth until half of his face is covered. The Maniac opens a prayer book and takes out a syringe, which he injects into Bertozzo; he then uses the rest on the Superintendent. As he and the journalist speak about bishops and scandals, Bertozzo picks up the portrait of the Queen hanging on the wall, writes on the back that the Maniac is a clinically deluded madman, and holds it up for the others to see. The Inspector tears the picture up and the Superintendent chastises the Inspector for destroying a royal portrait.

The Maniac continues to talk about scandals, arguing that they allow the public to vent their outrage without actually changing the system. Bertozzo, fed up, whips out a gun and threatens to shoot. He instructs the constable to handcuff the others to a horizontal bar at the back of the stage, then instructs the Maniac to tell the others who he really is. The Maniac brings out his files so that everyone will believe him; they read and are outraged. The Maniac then takes out the bomb that Bertozzo had left on the table. He instructs Bertozzo to drop the gun or he'll put his finger on the detonator and they'll all blow up. Bertozzo drops both the gun and the keys. The

Maniac reveals a tape recorder featuring all of their conversations, which he plans to copy and distribute to political entities and the media to cause a great scandal.

Suddenly the lights go out and the bomb explodes in the courtyard below. When the lights come back on, the Maniac is gone. Since the door is locked, they realize he must have left through the window. The Journalist slips her hand out of the handcuff and looks out the window; we can infer the Maniac has fallen to his death. She asks the Superintendent to make a statement. He begins, "Well, I had just left the room..." (86), but the journalist reminds him he was handcuffed here. The inspector points out that none of them had anything to do with the Maniac jumping, and the journalist says she may have to rethink her position about the anarchist's death. She leaves and the policemen take keys out of their pockets and unlock their handcuffs.

There is a knock on the door and the actor who played the Maniac enters the room, sporting a bushy black beard and a big belly. The policemen surround him, thinking he is the Maniac in another disguise; however, it turns out he is the actual High Court Judge, there to reopen the inquiry into the death of the anarchist.

Analysis

With the reappearance of Bertozzo, the momentum increases as the play approaches its climax. Bertozzo's goal to reveal the Maniac's identity is in direct opposition to the others' goals, leading each to act in more and more frantic ways. Each character interprets the Maniac's disguise differently, with only the audience - and the Maniac - comprehending the full truth of his identity and his multiple personas.

This segment of the play has a lot of knockabout violence and humor, with the policemen kicking, slapping, and gagging Bertozzo to keep him quiet. Aside from the obvious comic value, these actions represent the way in which bureaucrats assault the truth in order to maintain their power. The violence also reminds the audience that the anarchist was likely physically abused during his 72-hour detainment and interrogation.

The Maniac's disguise, once again, is symbolic. His wooden hand comes off twice, when shaken by the Inspector and then the Superintendent; this may symbolize the fact that they are eager to embrace a falsehood (the hand) if it benefits them, yet such falsehoods easily come undone. The second time, the Maniac switches the wooden male hand for a woman's hand, perhaps symbolizing the way in which falsehoods can so easily be procured and substituted for one another if one doesn't serve its purpose. Just as the woman's hand clearly doesn't fit on a man, however, falsehoods can be seen for what they are if we look carefully enough.

The discussion of undercover agents is more fully developed in this section as the Superintendent reveals that they have a few of their people planted in the audience. In so doing, Fo plays upon the fear created by the government's "strategy of tension" and the thought that informants really could be anywhere. At the same time, he makes use of the alienation effect by having the Maniac address the audience directly, saying, "Don't be alarmed, they're drama students. The real undercover ones are trained to sit quietly" (70). In so doing he destroys the fourth wall, that invisible barrier between actors and audience, and reminds the audience that they are watching a play. As such, their job is to think critically about the issues the play raises, rather than getting lost in the story that is being enacted on the stage.

Fo presents several pieces of counter-information in this part of the act: the fact that the bomb was so complex as to have been the work of professionals such as paramilitary organizations rather than disorganized anarchists, and the fact that the majority of bombings have been proven to be the work of fascists but blamed on far-left groups. As the facts implicate the government in the conspiracy, the play expands from commenting upon a single incident to making a statement about a much larger issue. The Piazza Fontana bombing, he implies, was part of the government's "strategy of tension," with the anarchist - and perhaps even the police - merely an unfortunate pawn.

The Maniac speaks passionately about scandals, contributing to a common debate in Italy in the 1970s between reform and revolution. Scandals, the Maniac explains, raise the public's opinions of the ruling establishment, for they lead to reforms (or the promise of reforms) that make the public think things are getting better without any real change taking place. Fo was a strong advocate of revolution, and he expressed his own views eloquently through the character of the Maniac. The list of scandals the Maniac uses to make his point changes based on the time and place of the performance, again reflecting Fo's belief that the play should be modified to speak to its audiences.

As the play nears its climax, the Maniac makes one more character change, this time impersonating a bishop. His choice of disguise allows Fo to include the church in his satire of institutions and suggests that the church, too, is the source of many lies.

There are several variations of endings for the play. This translation adopts the ending used in the original Italian version; afterwards, the "real" judge would sit down and have a discussion directly with the audience. It is ironic that the Maniac's surprise exit out the window leads the Journalist to rethink her opinion about the policemen's role in the anarchist's death; he succeeds at revealing the truth only to show, once again, how easily it can be manipulated. The ending implies that even if there were another inquiry into the anarchist's death, nothing would change; inquiries may cause scandals, but they don't change the system. In a later version, this point is reinforced with the Maniac's ending line: "The main thing is there'll be a thumping good scandal. So we can stand shoulder-to-shoulder in our social democracy and say, 'We are in the shit up to our necks, which is why we're walking with our heads held high.' (85)

In another variation, Fo offers two alternative endings and asks the audience to choose which they prefer: either the Journalist escapes and leaves the four policemen handcuffed and awaiting a ticking bomb, or she feels sorry for the men, uncuffs them, gets double-crossed and handcuffed herself, and is left to die. Which will prevail, this ending asks, truth or corruption?

Accidental Death of an Anarchist Symbols, Allegory and Motifs

the Maniac's false leg

Much of the Maniac's disguise as Captain Mark Weeny has symbolic value. The fake eye, hand, and leg all symbolize the lies told by the Maniac and embraced by the policemen. Bertozzo tries to undo the false leg and thereby expose the Maniac for who he really is, yet we learn that doing so is not enough: there are many layers of falsehoods in both his disguise and what he has been saying, and merely undoing one has little effect.

the Maniac's false eye

The Maniac's false eye may symbolize the idea that people are willing to "see" whatever they want to if it suits their purpose. The eye pops out when the Inspector slaps the Maniac on the back, suggesting that such lies are bound to become dislodged. A similar thing happens with the Maniac's false hand, which comes off when the Inspector and the Superintendent, both of whom embrace the lies, shake it. The Inspector later trips on the glass eye and falls over - a moment of slapstick humor that also suggests that his lies will hurt him in the end.

the open window

The window is a prominent part of the set, and the characters draw attention to it many times. The Maniac threatens to jump from the window if Bertozzo doesn't allow him to stay in the office, and he encourages the Superintendent and the Inspector to jump when they believe their culpability has been proven. On one level, the window is simply a reminder of what happened to the anarchist. On another, however, it may be a symbol of desperation. For instance, the Superintendent asks to close the window right after the Maniac points out the unbelievability of the stories they have been telling, perhaps sensing the trouble he is in.

the bomb

The bomb that Bertozzo brings to the office may symbolize the truth that the Maniac is trying to expose; if detonated, it could destroy the careers of the Inspector and the Superintendent just as the physical bomb could destroy their lives. The Maniac explains that the bomb is so complicated that it would be easy to hide a second timing device with a delayed action inside the first. So, too, is the truth complicated, hidden by layers upon layers of lies.

the tape recorder

The Journalist asks to use a tape recorder when she begins her inquisition. The Inspector hesitates, fearing that what they say could incriminate them, but the Maniac advises him to never say no. Later, the Maniac himself whips out a tape recorder, which has recorded the entire event. The Superintendent argues that the Maniac twisted everything they said and made them sound ridiculous, but the Maniac responds that it doesn't matter - it will still cause a scandal. The recorder may thus symbolize an incontrovertible truth, for the men cannot deny what has clearly been said.

Accidental Death of an Anarchist Metaphors and Similes

the Journalist as vulture

The Maniac compares the journalist to a vulture many times. When she asks why the Inspector is called the Window-Straddler and then later brings up the topic of undercover agents, he quietly says, "Fly away, come on, little vulture, nothing to see here." (58) As she nears the truth, asking how the anarchists could have pulled off such a complex operation without the police informants doing anything about the plan, he says, "Careful - vulture circling" (71). When she continues, noting that the inquiry judge himself thought the informant had lured the anarchists into an attack, he states, "The vulture has landed" (71). Vultures are birds that scavenge dead animals, although they may kill prey that is already in a weakened state. By using the term "vulture" to refer to the Journalist, the Maniac implies that the Inspector and the Superintendent are already "dead meat," the evidence clearly showing their culpability. Moreover, he implies that the Journalist has the power to destroy the two men through her exposition of the truth.

Bertozzo's slapstick

In Act Two, only Bertozzo knows the Maniac's true identity, yet he is silenced every time he tries to reveal it. The policemen's slapstick actions are a metaphor for the way in which the authorities cover up falsehoods. However, the truth cannot be silenced forever. When the Maniac injects Bertozzo with a tranquilizer, it has no effect, and eventually Bertozzo forces the others to listen to him. The fact that he needs a gun and handcuffs in order to do so suggests how difficult it can be to get people to believe the truth.

Switching the false hand for a woman's hand

The Maniac's wooden hand comes off two times, each time the result of being shaken by the Inspector or the Superintendent. Their eagerness to shake the false hand may symbolize their readiness to embrace a falsehood (the hand) if it benefits them, but those falsehoods can easily come undone. The second time the hand falls off, the Maniac replaces it with a woman's hand. By so doing, he may be demonstrating the ease with which falsehoods can be substituted for one another. Just as the woman's hand clearly doesn't fit a man, however, falsehoods can be recognized if observed carefully.

the Maniac's disguises

The Maniac's many disguises can be viewed as a metaphor for the multiple layers of truth. These disguises become more and more complex as the play approaches its climax. The journalist believes the Maniac is truly a bishop who had been masquerading as a forensics officer, while the Inspector and the Superintendent believe he is really a judge who pretended to be both a forensics officer and a bishop. Only Bertozzo knows that all three personas are false, yet he doesn't understand why his colleagues are going to such lengths to silence him. Each observer thinks he or she is in possession of the truth, but in fact nobody but the Maniac knows the entire story. The metaphor suggests that we, too, may still be deceived if we believe we possess knowledge others don't have.

insulting the Superintendent

The Maniac uses a simile when he tells the Superintendent, "Dealing with you is like doing one of those puzzle books bought by children and retards: 'Find the thirty-seven mistakes made by Inspector Barry Stupidhead'" (50). Such an insult incites derisive laughter towards the Superintendent while pointing out his many errors of judgment.

Accidental Death of an Anarchist Irony

Irony for satire

The Maniac uses irony throughout the play to satirize the official accounts of the anarchist's death given by the police. For instance, he points out the logical inconsistency of having a window wide open at midnight in December by saying the sun must not have set that evening. Similarly, he tries to reconcile the constable's account of having held onto one of the anarchist's shoes with witnesses' reports that the anarchist was wearing two shoes when he hit the pavement by asking if he were perhaps a triped.

Lying to reveal the truth

Since the Maniac's objective is to reveal the truth, it is ironic that he does so by lying, about both his identity and his intentions. He lies, too, about the trouble the Superintendent and the Inspector are in, leading them to actually consider jumping to their death out the window just as their own lies could have led the anarchist to commit suicide.

The Maniac's scandal

Several of the most powerful examples of situational irony occur as the play reaches its climax. The Maniac tells the others that he has recorded all of their conversations and will distribute the tape to political institutions and the media, thereby revealing the truth and causing a great scandal; yet moments earlier, he lectured at length on the uselessness of scandals for bringing about real change. Even more ironically, his surprise exit out the window at the end of the play causes the Journalist to rethink her prior opinion about the policemen's culpability in the anarchist's death. Thus, he succeeds at revealing the truth only to send the message that such a revelation does not guarantee the truth will be believed, nor that it will necessarily lead to positive change.

Accidental Death of an Anarchist Imagery

the open window

The open window is a reoccurring image, used to remind the audience of the issue at hand: uncovering the truth of what happened the night of the anarchist's death. The Maniac threatens to jump out the window if Bertozzo doesn't let him stay, and he asks to close the window when the Inspector arrives. The Superintendent, too, asks to close the window later on, providing a segue for the Maniac to point out the incongruity of having a window open at midnight in the middle of December. He even encourages the Inspector and the Superintendent to jump out of the open window to demonstrate how their deceptive interrogation techniques could have inspired the anarchist to do the same.

the Maniac's files

The Maniac's files contain documentation of his madness, as well as his "crimes" of impersonation. They appear at the beginning and the end of the play, both times to establish who the Maniac really is. As the play progresses his identity is disguised with layer upon layer of lies, until the files cause his entire charade to explode. It is telling that it is the Maniac's idea to share the files, understanding that the policemen and the Journalist would most likely not believe him without documentation to back up his story. Thus, even though it appears that Bertozzo has forced him to tell the others who he is, in actuality he wishes to dismantle the charade.

the exploding bomb

The bomb appears as the play approaches its climax, carried into the office by Bertozzo. It explodes immediately after the Maniac reveals his true identity, providing a powerful visual and auditory image that may symbolize the way in which the truth can violently erupt.

Accidental Death of an Anarchist Challenges of Translation

Accidental Death of an Anarchist has been performed in over 40 countries, yet translating and adapting the play has posed many challenges. First of all, it has been difficult to find a fixed text to translate. The play was rewritten many times during rehearsals, and Fo sometimes altered the script during performances based on the public's reaction or in response to current events. He tended to lose interest once the performance run was complete, leaving the task of presenting the script to a publisher to his wife, Franca Rame. Each of the three main published editions of the play include substantial changes, with further changes made for a version published in Fo's *Complete Works*.

There are considerable linguistic challenges as well. It can be difficult to translate words that may be either scientific or colloquial in Italian; thus, for instance, the term *manicomio* has been translated in different versions as *nuthouse, loony bin*, or *lunatic asylum*. There is a rhythm to some of the original language that cannot be captured in English; thus, the poetic sound of "*a me piace guidicare condannare reprimere perseguitare!*" loses its feel in the English: "I like judging, sentencing, going after people" (8). Sometimes Fo uses the structure of the language for a joke; for instance, he ends a sentence with one word (*la scarpa*, the shoe) and begins a new sentence with the same word, thus turning the tragedy of the event into a farce by paying irreverent attention to the shoe. While one can translate the literal meaning of the words, it is difficult to capture the comic undertones communicated by the original linguistic structure. Sometimes, too, translators miss the point in changing a grammatical structure. A close translation of the Maniac's statement about the anarchist's shoe would be, "And do you know what I say? I say that what the officer was left holding wasn't a shoe at all, it was a galosh," putting the emphasis on the speaker ("Do you know what *I* say? *I* say..."). The current translation loses some of this nuance: "So I put it to you that the constable had in his hands not a shoe, but a galosh" (53).

Another challenge is in maintaining the political focus of the play. In his run of performances, Fo would begin by talking about contemporary events, leading into a discussion of the origins and central lines of the play. He was also able to take for granted that his audience would have common background knowledge about the case and surrounding events in Italian political history. In an attempt to make the play as culturally relevant as possible, he encouraged translators to adapt references to events, change the setting, etc.; so, for instance, a British edition from 1980 refers to General Pinochet's 1973 coup in Chile, while Australian performances refer to Aboriginal deaths in police custody and attempts to blame left-wing groups for a 1978 bombing at the Sydney Hilton. However, translators occasionally went too far. For example, in the first production in Britain, adaptors Gillian Hanna and Gavin Richards took great liberties to modify the script as they saw fit. Richards cut out the Maniac's bishop disguise because he didn't understand Fo's rationale, and he even had the police admit to having pushed the anarchist out the window. Since it is unusual in British theater to have one dominant character do most of the talking, Richards modified the dialogue to reassign many of the Maniac's interruptions to other characters. Fo was unhappy with Richards' adaptation, believing it neglected the tragedy and politics of the original. American versions have often had the same problems in translation.

Later British translations have been more faithful in spirit to the original. Simon Nye's translation used for this study guide preserves Fo's original political intent and desire for relevance to a contemporary audience by setting the play in Britain and choosing references familiar to a British audience. As such, a modern audience can experience both the humor and the political vigor of the original, despite missing the linguistic nuances that are necessarily lost in translation.

Accidental Death of an Anarchist Literary Elements

Genre

Political drama, farce

Language

English (translated from Italian)

Setting and Context

Office in a police station; original setting was Milan, Italy; this translation is set in England. Time is "now." The play was originally performed in 1970, but references have been updated for later performances.

Narrator and Point of View

There is no narrator per se and therefore no point of view as traditionally defined. However, the audience views the action through the eyes of the Maniac. At one point he speaks to the audience, explaining his thoughts about impersonating a judge, and we understand that the Maniac is taking on various personas even as the characters on stage are fooled by his disguises.

Tone and Mood

The play is a farce, full of bawdy, slapstick humor. It is also political theater, which aims to engage the audience in understanding the tragedy of an innocent man's death while held in police custody. Thus the mood is light, but the comic interludes are interspersed between more serious moments of biting commentary on police and government corruption. Much of the humor is derived from satire, in which the Maniac makes fun of the police and exposes the ridiculousness of their story.

Protagonist and Antagonist

The Maniac is the protagonist, through whose eyes the audience sees the action unfold. The Inspector and his boss, the Superintendent, are the two primary antagonists.

Major Conflict

The Maniac wishes to expose the truth of what happened the night the anarchist fell to his death, while the police wish to exonerate themselves.

Climax

The climax occurs at the end of Act II, when Bertozzo pulls out a gun, handcuffs the others, and forces the Maniac to reveal his identity. After doing so, the Maniac takes control by threatening to blow everyone up with the bomb. He reveals a tape recorder that has taped their conversations, which he will share with the media and politicians to cause an enormous scandal. To everyone's surprise, he then jumps out the window and detonates the bomb in the courtyard.

Foreshadowing

The beginning of the play contains several moments of foreshadowing. When Bertozzo is surprised the Maniac has never played a judge before, the Maniac says he would like to; a few moments later, he gets his chance. The fact that he has impersonated a bishop three times may also foreshadow the fact that he will do so again. The Maniac engages in an ironic form of foreshadowing when he tells Bertozzo "I love it here with you, among policemen. I feel safe" (9). If the audience is not already familiar with the case of the anarchist, they will soon learn that being among policemen was anything but safe for Pinelli.

Understatement

N/A

Allusions

The entire play is an allusion to an event that occurred in Italy, even though the English version takes place in Britain. Many of the characters represent real-life people: the Inspector is Luigi Calabresi, the officer in charge of Pinelli's interrogation; the Superintendent is Marcello Guida, chief of police at the time; and the Journalist is Camilla Cederna, known for her in-depth reporting on controversial subjects. The play contains various other allusions to people and events. When the Maniac impersonated a psychiatrist and charged a family 200 pounds, his fee, he claimed, made the family think he was as good as Professor Anthony Clare, a psychiatrist on the radio and TV who engaged in a form of self-analysis with celebrities. He refers also to Freud, the founder of psychoanalysis; Mikhail Bakunin, founder of revolutionary anarchism; and Otto Weininger, a German author. Many allusions to current events have been changed in the translation. In this version, for instance, the Maniac asks the Inspector: "Is it true your boss used to run a mercenary outfit in Bosnia in the 1990s?" (12) In the original, Fo referenced instead an anti-fascist prison camp in southern Italy that had been run by Marcello Guida, chief of police.

Imagery

The open window is a recurring image, used to constantly bring attention back to the issue at hand: uncovering the truth of what happened the night the anarchist fell out of a fourth-story window while in police custody. The Maniac and the Superintendent both ask to shut the window at times, and the Maniac pushes the Inspector and the Superintendent towards the window after he demonstrates the desperation the anarchist likely felt while under interrogation.

Paradox

The character of the Maniac is a paradox of sorts: he is dedicated to revealing the truth, yet he does so through impersonating others and telling lies. His discourse on scandals reveals another paradox: is there really any value in revealing a scandalous truth if all it does is let the public vent their anger, then go on with their lives?

Parallelism

The Maniac, in his role as judge, interrogates the Inspector and the Superintendent in the same way that they interrogated the anarchist, telling them lies that led them to desperation just as they did to the anarchist.

Personification

Paradoxically, the Maniac can be thought of as a personification of reason and morality. Even the Journalist is motivated by her desire to get a good story, while the Maniac has no obvious ulterior motives behind his pursuit of truth. We see his desire for justice, too, when in Act I, Scene I he destroys the files of people he feels do not deserve to be punished while leaving those that do.

Use of Dramatic Devices

The play makes use of the alienation effect, a term coined by playwright Bertolt Brecht, in which the audience is hindered from identifying with the characters or getting immersed in the storyline. One technique by which Fo achieves this effect is having actors speak directly with the audience, thereby removing the invisible "fourth wall" between actors and audience and reminding audience members that they are watching a play. As a farce, the play also makes use of bawdy and slapstick humor. Fo believes that laughter allows people to feel anger without letting it dissipate, as it could in a tragedy where the audience cleanses themselves from negative emotions through tears. This type of humor is populist in nature, as it is accessible to everyone regardless of their level of education or economic class. The stage directions in the play are minimal. They were added after the fact by his wife, Franca Rame, who prepared most of Fo's plays for publication. Fo himself typically lost interest in a play once it was no longer being staged.

Accidental Death of an Anarchist Links

Dario Fo - Theatre Links

http://www.theatrelinks.com/dario-fo/

Links to a variety of resources on Fo, including photos and videos of him and his wife Franca Rame; links on *commedia dell'arte,* political theatre and satire; biographies; and interviews.

Dario Fo - Nobel Lecture

http://www.nobelprize.org/nobel_prizes/literature/laureates/1997/fo-lecture.html

Fo's acceptance speech for the 1997 Nobel Prize in Literature

Dario Fo: theater, painting, political satire

http://www.dariofo.it/

Dario Fo's official site. The site is written in Italian but can be translated into English using Google Translate.

Accidental Death of an Anarchist Suggested Essays

1. **Is the Maniac really mad?**

   Although the Maniac has been diagnosed with an "acting mania," his madness is merely a theatrical device. As an outsider, he sees the world differently than others and is thereby able to access hidden truths. Some might argue that the Maniac's passion for impersonation and deceiving others makes him mad, yet one could counter-argue that it is the Inspector and the Superintendent, so eager to believe the Maniac's lies if it serves their own interests, who are truly mad.

2. **How and why does Fo use the alienation effect?**

   The alienation effect, also known as the distancing effect, prevents the audience from identifying too closely with the characters or getting immersed in the storyline. One way Fo does this is by having characters speak directly to the audience. The Maniac does this as he tries on different types of judge personas, as does the Superintendent when he calls upon his "informants" seated in the audience to identify themselves. In this way Fo breaks the illusion of the "fourth wall," the imaginary barrier between actors and audience. Another technique is to include self-reflexive strategies, in which the play refers to itself as a play. The Maniac tells the audience that the Superintendent's "informants" are only drama students, and he likewise comments upon himself as an actor. By using these techniques, Fo undermines dramatic catharsis and entertainment value. He hopes to inspire his audience to think critically, engage in debate and consider different points of view.

3. **How does the translator make the play relevant to British audiences?**

   The translator uses idiomatic language and slang such as *tosspot, bird-witted ponce,* and *piss-taking* in order to appeal to the British non-elite. He also modified some cultural references, which maintains Fo's desire for the audience to think critically about the corruption or political machinations around them. For example, he has the Maniac ask if the Superintendent used to run a mercenary outfit in Bosnia, whereas in the original he asked if he ran an anti-fascist camp in the south of Italy. Similarly, the many scandals the Maniac names at the end of Act II were modified to appeal to British audiences.

4. **What kind of corruption does Fo target in the play?**

First and foremost, Fo targets corruption within the police force. The play brings to light the blatant lies told about the anarchist's case by the police, as well as questionable interrogation tactics such as the use of "psychological warfare" and, most likely, physical abuse. Fo also brings up the government's "strategy of tension", in which fascist or paramilitary groups engage in terrorist attacks that are blamed on far-left organizations. Finally, while he does not directly target the church, his choice of the Maniac's third disguise (the bishop) alludes to his belief that the church, too, is a source of hypocrisy and corruption.

5. **In what ways does the play follow the Italian theatre tradition of *commedia dell'arte*?**

In *commedia dell'arte*, a theatre tradition popular from the mid-16th to the mid-18th centuries, actors were at the heart of the playmaking process, improvising lines rather than precisely following a script. The sketches or scenes contained primarily of stock characters wearing masks depicting their archetype, the most celebrated of which was the Harlequin, or trickster. Fo, too, adapted his script often, changing lines in response to audience reactions or current events. Though most were based on real people, the play's roles are caricatures of sorts, given only non-specific names such as "Inspector", "Superintendent", or "Journalist". The Maniac is an updated version of the Harlequin, both a trickster who deceives the policemen through disguise and manipulation of language, and a clown whose ludicrous actions inspire raucous laughter. And, each of the Maniac's disguises could be considered a mask.

6. **What kind of humor does Fo use and why?**

Fo uses bawdy and slapstick humor as it appeals to all audiences - not just the elite. Bawdy humor is based on bodily functions, like when the Maniac pretends that Bertozzo has farted (blown a raspberry). Slapstick humor involves tripping, falling or mild, exaggerated violence, without any lasting harm. An example is when the Inspector punches Bertozzo in the face, thinking he had been making fun of him. Bertozzo is often at the receiving end of slapstick humor, as the others kick, slap, and gag him to keep him from revealing the Maniac's identity. These antics undercut the seriousness of the play's message, subverting the audience's expectations and engaging them.

7. **What are Fo's views on revolution, as expressed by the Maniac?**

Fo is an advocate of revolution, which involves a radical restructuring of society and its institutions. Like others on the far left, he sees reforms as mere band-aids, incapable of bringing about real change. The Maniac expresses this view in his discourse about scandals, explaining that scandals allow the government to placate the public through small reforms (or the promise of such reforms) without actually doing anything of value.

In fact, the people in power often manipulate scandals to distract the public and ensure that fundamental change does not occur.

8. **What kind of symbolism is present in the Maniac's disguise as Captain Mark Weeny?**

   The Maniac's fake eye, hand, and leg all symbolize the lies embraced by the policemen. The eye may symbolize the idea that people are willing to "see" whatever they want if it benefits them. The fact that it pops out when the Inspector slaps the Maniac on the back suggests such lies are tenuous and easily dislodged. Similarly, the Maniac's wooden hand comes off two times when shaken by one of the policemen. Their eagerness to grasp on to the Maniac may symbolize their readiness to embrace the lies; yet again, such lies easily come undone. By replacing the wooden hand with a woman's hand, the Maniac implies how easily one lie can be substituted for another. Finally, Bertozzo tries to undo the Maniac's false leg and thereby expose him for who he really is - leaving him quite literally with no leg to stand on. Yet there are many layers of falsehoods in both the Maniac's disguise and his words, and merely removing the disguises cannot undo the damage he has done in exposing the truth.

9. **How does the play suggest that there are many layers of truth or reality?**

   The play slowly reveals new evidence to build our understanding of what likely happened the night of the anarchist's death. For instance, it first appears that the anarchist jumped out the window in desperation as a result of the incriminating lies told by the Inspector and his men. However, the introduction of additional evidence - bruises on the anarchist's neck, the timing of the ambulance call, the incongruity of having a window open in December - suggests he may not have committed suicide at all, but rather was killed or severely injured by a blow to the neck. The Inspector is still culpable, but in a more direct and sinister way. The Maniac's impersonations serve as a metaphor for these layers of truth, with each character believing they know his true identity - which serves as yet another layer of disguise.

10. **How does Fo use the play to express his views on class oppression?**

    The Maniac touches upon this theme in his debate with the Journalist about the reliability of the three witnesses who confirmed the anarchist's alibi. The judge in the initial inquiry had dismissed the evidence of these witnesses as unreliable due to their age and likely disability. The Maniac points out that even if the judge's point is true and the witnesses' testimony cannot be trusted, it is because workers are so exploited that they cannot afford to take care of their health. At the same time, he implies that judges are prejudiced in that they evaluate witnesses' reliability based on apparent economic class.

Accidental Death of an Anarchist Quizzes

1. **In what language was the original play written?**
   A. Spanish
   B. Italian
   C. English
   D. French

2. **Which of the following characters were NOT modeled after an actual person?**
   A. the journalist
   B. the Maniac
   C. the Inspector
   D. the Superintendent

3. **Which character represents the officer who is thought to be responsible for the actual anarchist's death?**
   A. the Inspector
   B. Bertozzo
   C. the constable
   D. the Superintendent

4. **Which character is the protagonist?**
   A. the Inspector
   B. the Journalist
   C. the Superintendent
   D. the Maniac

5. **Which character serves primarily as the butt of derisive laughter?**
   A. the Superintendent
   B. the constable
   C. the Inspector
   D. Bertozzo

6. **How does the Maniac get into police headquarters at the beginning of the play?**
   A. He climbs in through the window.
   B. He is brought there under arrest with charges of impersonation.
   C. He walks in through the door.
   D. He is let in downstairs because they think he is a judge.

7. **What charge has been brought against the Maniac?**

A. murder
B. perjury
C. theft
D. impersonation

8. **Which of the following personae has the Maniac NOT assumed?**

A. psychiatrist
B. constable
C. bishop
D. surgeon

9. **What type of madness does the Maniac have?**

A. "acting mania"
B. bipolar disorder
C. schizophrenia
D. paranoia

10. **How much did the Maniac charge for a consultation as a phony psychiatrist?**

A. two hundred pounds
B. five hundred pounds
C. nothing; he offered his services for free
D. fifty pounds

11. **How did the Maniac learn about law?**

A. He reads a lot and picked it up.
B. He went to law school.
C. A clerk taught him in the lunatic asylum.
D. He studied in order to impersonate a lawyer.

12. **Why does the Maniac think it is great to be a judge?**

A. They never retire and gain more responsibility as they age.
B. They get paid a lot.
C. They get to wear a robe to work.
D. They get to decide people's fates.

13. **On what floor is Bertozzo's office?**

A. the fourth
B. the first
C. the third
D. the fourteenth

14. **What does the Maniac threaten to do if Bertozzo makes him leave?**

A. throw himself down the stairs
B. report him to his superior
C. jump out the window
D. handcuff him to the wall

15. **Why does the Maniac reenter the room after Bertozzo leaves?**
   A. He wants to destroy all the files.
   B. He is looking for evidence.
   C. He wants to jump out the window.
   D. To get his paperwork.

16. **The anarchist fell out of a window on which floor?**
   A. the fourteenth
   B. the fourth
   C. the first
   D. the third

17. **Why does the Inspector call Bertozzo's office?**
   A. To remind him that he has a meeting with Forensics.
   B. To request the Maniac's files.
   C. To ask him about the bomb.
   D. To tell him a judge is being sent to reopen the inquiry into the anarchist's death.

18. **What reason does the Maniac give for Bertozzo laughing while he talks to the Inspector on the phone?**
   A. because of the trouble the superintendent and the inspector are in
   B. because he wants to get in a fight
   C. because the Maniac has just told a joke
   D. because he has just blown a raspberry

19. **What does the Maniac insinuate that the Inspector's boss used to do?**
   A. sell military secrets to Russia
   B. run a mercenary outfit in Bosnia
   C. run a Nazi concentration camp
   D. work as a judge

20. **What disrespectful thing does the Maniac say Bertozzo is doing?**
   A. blowing a raspberry
   B. laughing at the trouble the Inspector is in
   C. joking that the Inspector will be relocated to an office in the basement
   D. all of the above

21. **What does the Inspector say he will do to Bertozzo?**
   A. fire him
   B. report him to his superior
   C. kick him in the shin
   D. punch him in the face

22. **What disguise does the Maniac decide to take on first?**

A. a forensics officer

B. a surgeon

C. a judge

D. a bishop

23. **Where does the Maniac get the clothing for his judge disguise?**

A. He doesn't put on any special clothes.

B. He takes Bertozzo's coat and hat off a clothes rack.

C. He disappears behind a desk and reappears in costume.

D. He finds them in his bag.

24. **What does the Maniac warn Bertozzo about?**

A. The Inspector is looking for him to punch him in the face.

B. The Inspector is about to blow him a raspberry.

C. A judge will be arriving shortly to interview the policemen.

D. The high court is reopening the inquiry into the death of the anarchist.

25. **What happened to the charge sheets in Bertozzo's office?**

A. The Maniac threw them away.

B. They are still hidden in his desk.

C. The Maniac took them with him.

D. The Maniac tore them up.

Quiz 1 Answer Key

1. **(B)** Italian
2. **(B)** the Maniac
3. **(A)** the Inspector
4. **(D)** the Maniac
5. **(D)** Bertozzo
6. **(A)** He climbs in through the window.
7. **(D)** impersonation
8. **(B)** constable
9. **(A)** "acting mania"
10. **(A)** two hundred pounds
11. **(C)** A clerk taught him in the lunatic asylum.
12. **(A)** They never retire and gain more responsibility as they age.
13. **(C)** the third
14. **(C)** jump out the window
15. **(D)** To get his paperwork.
16. **(B)** the fourth
17. **(D)** To tell him a judge is being sent to reopen the inquiry into the anarchist's death.
18. **(A)** because of the trouble the superintendent and the inspector are in
19. **(B)** run a mercenary outfit in Bosnia
20. **(D)** all of the above
21. **(D)** punch him in the face
22. **(C)** a judge
23. **(B)** He takes Bertozzo's coat and hat off a clothes rack.
24. **(A)** The Inspector is looking for him to punch him in the face.
25. **(D)** The Maniac tore them up.

Accidental Death of an Anarchist Quizzes

1. **What hangs on the back wall of the office?**
   A. the Inspector's police credentials
   B. a painting of the Virgin Mary
   C. nothing
   D. a portrait of the Queen of England

2. **Why does the Inspector massage his hand?**
   A. His hands are cold.
   B. He has a nervous tic.
   C. He hurt his hand punching Bertozzo.
   D. He caught his hand in the door.

3. **What does the Maniac say happens when someone lies to him?**
   A. His hand hurts and he has to rub it.
   B. His neck twitches.
   C. His nose itches.
   D. He gets terribly angry and punches them.

4. **Why doesn't the Maniac want to go to the Superintendent's office?**
   A. The incident with the anarchist took place in his room.
   B. He doesn't want Bertozzo to see him as they change offices.
   C. The Maniac prefers the third floor.
   D. It is too far away.

5. **Why does the Inspector want to find Bertozzo?**
   A. He wants to punch him again.
   B. The Superintendent has asked for him.
   C. Bertozzo was present at the anarchist's death and should be part of the inquiry.
   D. Bertozzo has the paperwork regarding the anarchist's death.

6. **Why is the Superintendent upset with the Inspector?**
   A. The Inspector punched Bertozzo in the face.
   B. The Inspector has been disrespectful.
   C. The Inspector sent an order for the Superintendent to come, even though the Superintendent is his superior.
   D. all of the above

7. **Who do the Superintendent and the Inspector think they are talking to when they meet the Maniac?**
   A. Captain Mark Weeny from Forensic
   B. Bishop Bernard, police liaison officer and consultant
   C. Lord Justice Malcolm, first counsel to the High Court
   D. Professor Anthony Rabbi, Psychiatrist

8. **At what time did the interrogation of the anarchist begin?**
   A. noon
   B. midnight
   C. 8:00pm
   D. dawn

9. **What was the anarchist's job?**
   A. construction worker
   B. railway shunter
   C. banker
   D. He was unemployed.

10. **According to the policemen, why did the anarchist fall out the window?**
    A. He had a sudden "raptus" and jumped.
    B. He wanted to make a fool of the policemen and committed suicide in order to do so.
    C. The Inspector had him sit on the window ledge during the interrogation and he accidentally fell.
    D. One of the constables got angry and pushed him.

11. **What is a "raptus," according to the police reports?**
    A. A kind of suicidal anguish which can strike people when provoked to extreme anxiety or desperation.
    B. A state of hyper-alert attention.
    C. A kind of disease in which the patient thinks he can fly out of windows.
    D. A feeling of oneness with God.

12. **What did the Superintendent accuse the anarchist of doing?**
    A. planning to assassinate the prime minister
    B. bombing the Memorial to the Unknown Soldier
    C. planting bombs at the railway station
    D. trying to undermine the government by spreading false rumors

13. **What did the Inspector tell the anarchist about the bombing?**

A. The anarchist's friend had turned him in.

B. He had indisputable proof that the anarchist was single-handedly responsible for the bombings.

C. Another member of their anarchist group, a dancer, had confessed to planting the bomb at the bank.

D. They had video footage of the bombings implicating the anarchist and his comrade.

14. **What was the anarchist's alibi?**

A. He was dancing with his girlfriend.

B. He was gambling with some old-age pensioners.

C. He was taking care of his grandfather.

D. He was playing cards.

15. **Why didn't the judge accept the witnesses' testimony that the anarchist's alibi was true?**

A. They all had conflicting versions of events.

B. They were old-age pensioners and therefore "unreliable".

C. He believed the anarchist had bribed them to confirm his story.

D. They were all senile.

16. **How did the police know the anarchist dancer bombed the bank?**

A. The anarchist dancer confessed to everything during his interrogation.

B. They didn't; they made up his confession.

C. Everything was recorded on the bank's security camera.

D. Witnesses saw the anarchist dancer plant the bomb.

17. **What does the Maniac recommend the Superintendent and the Inspector do when they think they are in trouble?**

A. find new jobs as car-park attendants

B. jump out the window

C. give the Maniac a bribe to keep the story quiet

D. issue a full confession

18. **According to the Superintendent, whose fault is it that the police are in trouble?**

A. the government's

B. the Inspector's

C. the anarchist's

D. the Maniac's

19. **What did the Superintendent change in his second version of events?**

A. the time the anarchist's interrogation began
B. the time the anarchist jumped out the window
C. the reason the anarchist jumped
D. the time the ambulances arrived

20. **According to the second version of events, why did the anarchist calm down?**

A. The Inspector admitted that he had lied about the anarchist dancer's confession.
B. Everyone sang a song together.
C. He had a cigarette, which helped him relax.
D. He said he didn't get along well with the anarchist dancer anymore.

21. **What did the constable supposedly do to make the anarchist feel better?**

A. gave him a hug
B. gave him a pat on the cheek
C. gave him a stick of chewing gum
D. gave him a cigarette

22. **What does the Maniac propose the Superintendent did to make the anarchist feel better?**

A. put a friendly hand on his shoulder
B. pat him on the cheek
C. give him a cigarette
D. say "Don't lose heart - you wait, anarchy will never die"

23. **According to the Maniac, what did the Inspector do to make the anarchist feel better?**

A. say "Don't lose heart - you wait, anarchy will never die"
B. pat him on the cheek
C. sing a song
D. all of the above

24. **What is the primary reason the Maniac gives for having the men sing a song with the anarchist?**

A. It would explain why the anarchist jumped.
B. It would raise the public's opinion of them.
C. It actually happened.
D. It would make their story more believable.

25. **What did the Inspector say to the anarchist's widow when she asked why nobody had told her of her husband's death?**

   A. "Sorry, it won't happen again."
   B. "What? Nobody told you?"
   C. "I'm so sorry. How terrible this must be for you."
   D. "Don't lose heart - you wait, anarchy will never die!"

Quiz 2 Answer Key

1. **(D)** a portrait of the Queen of England
2. **(C)** He hurt his hand punching Bertozzo.
3. **(B)** His neck twitches.
4. **(A)** The incident with the anarchist took place in his room.
5. **(D)** Bertozzo has the paperwork regarding the anarchist's death.
6. **(D)** all of the above
7. **(C)** Lord Justice Malcolm, first counsel to the High Court
8. **(C)** 8:00pm
9. **(B)** railway shunter
10. **(A)** He had a sudden "raptus" and jumped.
11. **(A)** A kind of suicidal anguish which can strike people when provoked to extreme anxiety or desperation.
12. **(C)** planting bombs at the railway station
13. **(C)** Another member of their anarchist group, a dancer, had confessed to planting the bomb at the bank.
14. **(D)** He was playing cards.
15. **(B)** They were old-age pensioners and therefore "unreliable".
16. **(B)** They didn't; they made up his confession.
17. **(B)** jump out the window
18. **(A)** the government's
19. **(B)** the time the anarchist jumped out the window
20. **(D)** He said he didn't get along well with the anarchist dancer anymore.
21. **(C)** gave him a stick of chewing gum
22. **(A)** put a friendly hand on his shoulder
23. **(D)** all of the above
24. **(B)** It would raise the public's opinion of them.
25. **(A)** "Sorry, it won't happen again."

Accidental Death of an Anarchist Quizzes

1. **What does the Maniac say is the reason the Superintendent had nothing to do with the anarchist's death?**
   A. He wasn't there.
   B. He called the ambulance, so he must have been trying to save the anarchist.
   C. He sang a song with the anarchist, so clearly the two were friends.
   D. None of the above

2. **How many policemen were in the room when the anarchist fell to his death?**
   A. four
   B. two
   C. six
   D. five

3. **What were the policemen supposedly doing with the anarchist between 8:00pm and midnight?**
   A. Telling him lies about the anarchist dancer
   B. Threatening to push him out the window
   C. Playing cards with him
   D. Questioning him in a "jokey manner"

4. **What was one of the anarchist dancer's jobs?**
   A. sewing beads onto Liberty lampshades
   B. editing a communist magazine
   C. working at a strip club
   D. laying down railroad tracks

5. **What is the Maniac's explanation for why the window was open the night the anarchist died?**
   A. The anarchist had been smoking and they opened the window to get some fresh air.
   B. It was an unusually warm winter's night.
   C. The sun didn't set.
   D. It was a hot evening in early July.

6. **In what month did the incident with the anarchist take place?**
   A. September
   B. July
   C. December
   D. February

7. **What else is fishy about the window, besides the fact that it was open?**
   A. It was exceedingly small, so it would have been hard for the anarchist to fit through without help.
   B. It was high up on the wall, so it would have been hard for the anarchist to jump out without help.
   C. It had no shutters.
   D. All of the above

8. **What supposedly happened when the constable caught the anarchist's foot?**
   A. The anarchist dangled out the window until the constable couldn't hold on any longer.
   B. The anarchist's shoe came off in the constable's hand.
   C. The anarchist kicked him in the face.
   D. None of the above

9. **What is the Maniac's explanation for why witnesses said the anarchist was wearing two shoes when he landed?**
   A. He had three feet.
   B. The constable put the shoe back onto the anarchist mid-flight.
   C. He was also wearing a galosh, which came off in the constable's hand.
   D. All of the above

10. **What is the Journalist's name?**
    A. Maria Felkin
    B. Mark Weeny
    C. Camilla Cederna
    D. none of the above

11. **Who does the Maniac first disguise himself as when the journalist arrives?**
    A. Lord Justice Malcolm, first counsel to the High Court
    B. Captain Mark Weeny, Head of Forensic
    C. Constable Chester
    D. Bishop Bernard, police liaison officer and consultant

12. **Which of the following is NOT part of the Maniac's disguise?**
    A. a wooden hand
    B. a false moustache
    C. a false beard
    D. a black eye-patch

13. **What is the Inspector's nickname?**
    A. Inspector Gadget
    B. Inspector Throws-Anarchists-out-the-Window
    C. the Window-Straddler
    D. Captain Underpants

14. **To which bird does the Maniac compare the Journalist?**

A. a hawk
B. a parrot
C. an eagle
D. a vulture

15. **Why does the Journalist point out that the inquiry failed to include the report on the anarchist's body's trajectory?**

A. It would have shown whether or not the Inspector shot him before he fell.
B. It would have shown whether he jumped or someone pushed him out the window.
C. It would have shown whether or not he was still alive when he emerged from the window.
D. None of the above

16. **When did the ambulance receive a phone call from the police?**

A. three minutes past midnight
B. twenty minutes before midnight
C. two minutes before midnight
D. at exactly midnight

17. **Why does it matter when the ambulance was called?**

A. The call came in five minutes after the anarchist supposedly jumped, showing that the police were trying to help.
B. It doesn't matter at all.
C. The call came in an hour before the anarchist supposedly jumped, showing that something fishy was going on.
D. The call came in five minutes before the anarchist supposedly jumped, showing that something fishy was going on.

18. **What did the Inspector blame for the discrepancy between the time the ambulance was called and the time the anarchist jumped?**

A. faulty records
B. good foresight
C. inaccurate timepieces
D. all of the above

19. **What was unusual about the dead anarchist's body?**

A. He was wearing a galosh over one of his shoes.
B. He had a wooden hand.
C. He had bruises on his neck.
D. He had a black eye.

20. **What best explains the evidence brought up by the Journalist?**

A. One of the men interrogating the anarchist whacked him on his neck and injured him.
B. The anarchist called the ambulance before jumping out the window in case he survived.
C. The anarchist hit his neck as he jumped out the window.
D. none of the above

21. **What did the report on the trajectory of the anarchist's body out the window reveal?**

A. The anarchist leaped out of the window with a lot of force.
B. The anarchist was already dead when he fell.
C. The anarchist's neck was snapped when he fell.
D. The anarchist was still alive until he hit the ground.

22. **How did the public prosecutor classify the anarchist's death?**

A. a murder
B. an "accidental death"
C. a suicide
D. none of the above

23. **What does the Maniac accidentally swallow?**

A. his glass eye
B. some dirty water
C. a termite
D. the Inspector's ring

24. **What genre of play is Accidental Death of an Anarchist?**

A. operetta
B. farce
C. historical drama
D. commedia dell'arte

25. **Which character is based on Luigi Calabresi from the play's real-life inspiration, the Pinelli case?**

A. the Maniac
B. Bertozzo
C. the Journalist
D. the Inspector

Quiz 3 Answer Key

1. **(A)** He wasn't there.
2. **(C)** six
3. **(D)** Questioning him in a "jokey manner"
4. **(A)** sewing beads onto Liberty lampshades
5. **(C)** The sun didn't set.
6. **(C)** December
7. **(B)** It was high up on the wall, so it would have been hard for the anarchist to jump out without help.
8. **(B)** The anarchist's shoe came off in the constable's hand.
9. **(D)** All of the above
10. **(A)** Maria Felkin
11. **(B)** Captain Mark Weeny, Head of Forensic
12. **(C)** a false beard
13. **(C)** the Window-Straddler
14. **(D)** a vulture
15. **(C)** It would have shown whether or not he was still alive when he emerged from the window.
16. **(C)** two minutes before midnight
17. **(D)** The call came in five minutes before the anarchist supposedly jumped, showing that something fishy was going on.
18. **(C)** inaccurate timepieces
19. **(C)** He had bruises on his neck.
20. **(A)** One of the men interrogating the anarchist whacked him on his neck and injured him.
21. **(B)** The anarchist was already dead when he fell.
22. **(B)** an "accidental death"
23. **(A)** his glass eye
24. **(B)** farce
25. **(D)** the Inspector

Accidental Death of an Anarchist Quizzes

1. **Why does Bertozzo come back?**
   A. He forgot his coat.
   B. He wants to get revenge for the Inspector punching him in the eye.
   C. He wants to arrest the Maniac.
   D. He has a replica of the bomb that exploded at the bank.

2. **How does Bertozzo know that the Maniac isn't really Captain Mark Weeny?**
   A. Bertozzo knows the real Captain Mark Weeny.
   B. There is no Captain Mark Weeny.
   C. Bertozzo recognizes the Maniac right away.
   D. He doesn't know; he believes the disguise.

3. **What is one of Bertozzo's specialties?**
   A. forensics
   B. explosives
   C. ammunition
   D. handcuffs

4. **Why was it a problem that the police blew up the bomb that didn't go off on its own?**
   A. It destroyed evidence that could have revealed who planted the bomb.
   B. It injured 19 people.
   C. It did not belong to them.
   D. It made it difficult to build a replica.

5. **How does the Maniac explain why the police blew up the bomb?**
   A. There may be a delayed reaction trigger that could have detonated the bomb while in custody.
   B. The device was complicated and could not be safely disconnected.
   C. The device was poorly made and might have killed anyone who touched it.
   D. all of the above

6. **Why is it significant that the bomb was complex?**
   A. Assembling or handling such a bomb requires professional expertise that the anarchists don't possess.
   B. It explains why the policemen blew it up.
   C. Such a bomb could only have been procured from the military, suggesting that a soldier was responsible.
   D. none of the above

7. **How many members of the anarchist group were actually police informants?**
   A. four of twelve
   B. two of ten
   C. four of ten
   D. two of twelve

8. **What is the purpose of police informers and spies?**
   A. They carry out atrocities to give the police an excuse for a clampdown.
   B. They help the police to control political groups.
   C. They provide an early-warning system.
   D. all of the above

9. **What is the Superintendent's excuse for why his informer didn't stop the anarchist from planting a bomb?**
   A. The informer tried to stop the bombing but was unsucessful.
   B. The anarchists discovered the informer's true identity and disposed of him.
   C. The informer was absent from the group in the days before the bombing.
   D. The informer tried to let the Superintendent know about the plan, but the phones weren't working.

10. **Of 173 bomb attacks to date, how many have been proven to be the work of fascists?**
    A. 98
    B. none of them
    C. 172
    D. 102

11. **Of 173 bomb attacks to date, how many were made to look like the work of far-left groups?**
    A. a few of them
    B. none of them
    C. almost all of them
    D. all of them

12. **Who most likely planted the bombs?**
   A. anarchists
   B. fascist and paramilitary organizations
   C. the police themselves
   D. Communists

13. **According to the Maniac, what is the purpose of scandals?**
   A. to satisfy the public's desire to expose corruption without actually causing real change
   B. to keep journalists in business
   C. to incite the public to start a revolution
   D. to bring about much-needed reforms

14. **Why does the Maniac change disguise a third time?**
   A. Bertozzo has made it clear that he isn't Captain Mark Weeny.
   B. He finds it entertaining.
   C. He decides to reveal his true identity.
   D. His prior disguise was falling apart.

15. **What is the Maniac's third disguise?**
   A. a bishop
   B. a forensics officer
   C. a constable
   D. a psychiatrist

16. **What does the Inspector put in Bertozzo's mouth?**
   A. the bishop's ring
   B. a glass eye
   C. a gag
   D. a rubber stamp

17. **What is the effect of the tranquilizer the Maniac gives to Bertozzo?**
   A. It makes him docile.
   B. It keeps him from talking.
   C. It knocks him out.
   D. It has no effect.

18. **What does Bertozzo use to write his message about the Maniac?**
   A. the Superintendent's diploma
   B. a portrait of the Queen of England
   C. an envelope containing the police report from the initial inquiry
   D. a pad of paper

19. **What does the Inspector do in response to Bertozzo's message?**

A. He tears up the portrait of the Queen.
B. He punches him in the face.
C. He yanks off the Maniac's false leg.
D. He gags him with a rubber stamp.

20. **Why does Bertozzo handcuff the others?**

A. He is angry at the way he has been treated and wants to get revenge.
B. It is the only way they will listen to the truth.
C. He and the Maniac are working together to blow up the others.
D. all of the above

21. **How does the Maniac get the others to believe who he really is?**

A. He writes his name on a piece of paper.
B. He takes off his disguise and tells them.
C. He swears on a Bible.
D. He shows them his clinical records.

22. **What does the Inspector want to do when he finds out who the Maniac really is?**

A. arrest him
B. push him out the window
C. physically assault him
D. make the Journalist publish an article about him

23. **What is the Maniac planning to do with the tape recorder?**

A. make copies of the tape and send it to newspapers and political institutions
B. give it to the Journalist
C. blackmail the police to confess
D. blow it up

24. **What happens when the lights go out?**

A. The police and the Journalist are confused.
B. The bomb goes off in the courtyard.
C. The Maniac jumps out the window.
D. all of the above

25. **Who is the bearded man who enters at the end of the last scene?**

A. the Maniac
B. the anarchist
C. the judge sent to reopen the inquiry into the death of the anarchist
D. the Superintendent's superior

Some of these are not in my edition

Quiz 4 Answer Key

1. **(D)** He has a replica of the bomb that exploded at the bank.
2. **(A)** Bertozzo knows the real Captain Mark Weeny.
3. **(B)** explosives
4. **(A)** It destroyed evidence that could have revealed who planted the bomb.
5. **(A)** There may be a delayed reaction trigger that could have detonated the bomb while in custody.
6. **(A)** Assembling or handling such a bomb requires professional expertise that the anarchists don't possess.
7. **(B)** two of ten
8. **(D)** all of the above
9. **(C)** The informer was absent from the group in the days before the bombing.
10. **(D)** 102
11. **(C)** almost all of them
12. **(B)** fascist and paramilitary organizations
13. **(A)** to satisfy the public's desire to expose corruption without actually causing real change
14. **(A)** Bertozzo has made it clear that he isn't Captain Mark Weeny.
15. **(A)** a bishop
16. **(D)** a rubber stamp
17. **(D)** It has no effect.
18. **(B)** a portrait of the Queen of England
19. **(A)** He tears up the portrait of the Queen.
20. **(B)** It is the only way they will listen to the truth.
21. **(D)** He shows them his clinical records.
22. **(C)** physically assault him
23. **(A)** make copies of the tape and send it to newspapers and political institutions
24. **(D)** all of the above
25. **(C)** the judge sent to reopen the inquiry into the death of the anarchist

Accidental Death of an Anarchist Bibliography

Kristin Sherwood, author of ClassicNote. Completed on November 20, 2014, copyright held by GradeSaver.

Updated and revised by Christine McKeever December 27, 2014. Copyright held by GradeSaver.

Fo, Dario. Ed. Joseph Farrell. Trans. Simon Nye. Accidental Death of an Anarchist. London: Bloomsbury, 2005.

Tom Behan. Dario Fo: Revolutionary Theatre. London: Pluto Press, 2000.

"Accidental Death of an Anarchist." *Drama for Students*. Ed. Sara Constantakis. Vol. 23. Detroit: Gale, 2006. Online.

Cairns, Christopher. "Dario Fo: Overview." *Contemporary World Writers*. Ed. Tracy Chevalier. 2nd ed. Detroit: St. James Press, 1993. Online.

Fitzpatrick, Tim and Ksenia Sawczak. "Accidental Death of a Translator: The Difficult Case of Dario Fo." *About Performance* 1 (1993): 15-34. Online.

Dell'Amico, Carol. "Critical Essay on 'Accidental Death of an Anarchist'." *Drama for Students*. Ed. Sara Constantakis. Vol. 23. Detroit: Gale, 2006. *Literature Resource Center*. Online.

Boothman, Derek. "Popular and Political Theatre: An interview with Dario Fo." *Marxism Today* (August 1983): 37-39. Online.

"Dario Fo." *Contemporary Authors Online*. Detroit: Gale, 2007. *Literature Resource Center*. Online.

Essay Accidental Death of an Anarchist as a Play of Social and Political Comment

by Shaleen Attre

Dario Fo, author of Accidental Death of an Anarchist, won the Nobel Prize for literature in 1997 and the Swedish Academy while awarding him the prize noted that Fo's "works are open for creative additions, dislocations, continually encouraging actors to improvise". Fo has always wanted his plays to be improvised and adapted in keeping with the environment and the conditions of performance. This is why he encouraged adaptations instead of translations of his scripts into other languages as long as it suits the socio-economic / cultural context of performance with the political thrust not being undermined or distorted. From the beginning he has sought to develop a kind of theatre which does not merely reflect documents but actively participates in the collective life and struggles of his audiences and becomes a form of collaborative political action.

The reason for Fo's immense success and his ability to evoke the kind of audience response as he did in Italy is not just the artistic vitality of his theatre but also the political immediacy of the matters he addresses in his plays like Accidental Death of an Anarchist, which essentially becomes a performance-centred rather than script-centred text. Javed Mallick has identified one main problem with analyzing the play as a classroom text, being the fact that the play works in performance only if it is related to an immediate political context and situation familiar to the audiences and performers. According to him Fo originally wrote the play as a political intervention into a specific situation and we should, therefore, accordingly analyse it keeping in that troubled fascist state / anarchist period in mind.

Fo had essentially based his play on the bombing in Piazza Fontana in 1969 and the subsequent death of the arrested anarchist, Pinelli, who fell from a fourth floor window to a courtyard below. The room he was being questioned in was just 13 by 11 feet and there were five experienced officers in the room when Pinelli 'flew' from the window with a 'cat-like jump'. The first police explanation was that Pinelli had committed suicide, insisting that the leap was proof of his guilt. However, many other theories cropped up owing to the lack of physical evidence on the body, as brought out in the play, among which were the act of blatant murder by the police or of an 'accidental' death owing to negligence and extreme intimidation techniques being deployed by the police. Fo, in the guise of the madman disguised as the examining magistrate, points out the grotesquely farcical lengths to which the Italian police went to exonerate themselves from any responsibility for Pinelli's death and to justify not following up any right wing leads in their investigation of the Piazza

Fontana bombs. The bombs were in fact subsequently proved to be the work of two fascists.

At this juncture it becomes imperative to talk about the 'strategy of tension'. The thinking behind the strategy of tension, whether it be the neo fascist groups who planted a whole series of bombs in those years or their accomplices and protectors within the secret services and the state machinery was to halt the growth in the strength of the working class. The placing of bombs randomly was done to create severe tension within the society. It was important for these forces to create the impression that it was anarchists, communists, trade unionists and so on who were behind the bombs. It was hoped that the overall situation which would be created would be one in which it would be unclear who was specifically responsible, so in order to stop the chaos, the left had to be suppressed in general. As Tom Behan puts it, in the climate of fear and revulsion created by the bombings it would be relatively easier for the state to justify the suspension of normal democratic procedures and subjugation of the left. Apart from this, the ultimate goal was the creation of a political system akin to fascism, which is why the involvement of fascist groups and elements within secret services with fascist sympathies became crucial.

The play's audience was aware of the gravity of the 'strategy of tension' and it is a direct reflection of Fo's achievement that he was able to put forth the play like a madcap farce and popular comedy distancing the tragic implications in 'order to forestall the audience's empathy.' This strategy is embodied in the many disguise changes that the madman undertakes.

In the British adaptations of this play the police characters have been turned into mere caricatures, which was exceedingly disturbing for Fo. Thus, it becomes vital to stress that they are not intended as caricatures or stereotypes, making not only the British but several other foreign productions inaccurate. There is no doubt that Fo makes them, as Tony Mitchell says, 'the butt of comedy and farce'. This is, however, inherent to the statements and behavior of devious, dangerous types who show the abuses of power that the police ruthlessly exerted in their extreme takedown of the Italian Left. On the other hand, Fo does not advocate or show any sympathy to the anarchists, whom he depicts as an insignificant group of extremists whose organization was so chaotic that they could not have possibly been the perpetrators of something so complex as the Fontana bombings, which the inspector also admitted required 'military precision'. The play's indictment of police behaviour takes on a more serious note in the character of Felletti, who seems to be unrelenting about the embarrassing facts of the Pinelli scandal. However, Tony Mitchell argues that her hard line of questioning was balanced by the madman's change in disguise, filled with artificial limbs, from the examining magistrate into, 'Captain Marcantonio Piccini from forensic research'. In an interesting insight, however, Jolynn Wing observes that 'Fo incarnates Piccini as a preposterous conglomeration of such blatant bogus body parts that he is transposed into a virtual marionette… As the scene builds up, it becomes increasingly evident that the grotesquely corrupted body of the Maniac and the body politic are theatrical reflections of each other'.

The farcical capers of the play's situation reach a climax when the Maniac is stripped of his 'forensic disguise' and proceeds to impersonate the Bishop, who is collaborating with the police. This disguise enabled Fo to satirize the Church and discuss consequences of the affair which as the Bishop states, is used as 'the fertilizer of social democracy'. As said before, Fo rendered performance-oriented plays. Therefore, by leaving the ending unresolved, the play did not have any catharsis or outlet for the audience, which Fo hoped would stimulate a desire for political change. Discussions after the play tended to deal with the need for a revolutionary strategy and a 'counter power' developed on Marxist Leninist lines against the Christian Democrat state.

As Fo later wrote in the preface to a sequel to the play, 'this monstrous tragic farce which goes under the name of 'state massacre', presented courtesy of the democratic organs of the state had the programmed result of a vast 'isolation campaign' of workers struggles and the obliteration of their more militant activists'. It was written as a response to a particular, critical political moment and requires the same sensitivity to immediate politics in production.

Bibliography -:

? Contextualizing Fo: Radical Theatre of the 1960's by Javed Mallick. A critical companion to Accidental Death of an Anarchist. Worldview, 2006.

? La Commune and Accidental Death of an Anarchist by Tony Mitchell. Dario Fo: People's Court Jester. London and Ny., Methuen, 1984.

? Accidental Death of an Anarchist by Tom Behan. Dario Fo: Revolutionary Theatre. London: Pluto, 2000.

ClassicNotes

GradeSaver™

Getting you the grade since 1999™

Other ClassicNotes from GradeSaver™

ClassicNotes

GradeSaver™

Getting you the grade since 1999™

ClassicNotes

GradeSaver™

Getting you the grade since 1999™

Other ClassicNotes from GradeSaver™

The Vicar of Wakefield
The Visit
The Wars
The Waste Land
The Wave
The Wealth of Nations
The White Devil
The White Tiger
The Wind in the Willows
The Winter's Tale
The Woman Warrior
The Wonderful Wizard of Oz
The Yellow Wallpaper
The Zoo Story
Things Fall Apart
Three Cups of Tea
Three Men in a Boat (To Say Nothing of the Dog)
Through the Looking Glass
Thus Spoke Zarathustra
Titus Andronicus
To Build a Fire
To Kill a Mockingbird
Top Girls
To the Lighthouse
Touching Spirit Bear
Treasure Island
Trifles
Troilus and Cressida
Tropic of Cancer
Tropic of Capricorn
Tuesdays With Morrie
Twelfth Night
Twilight
Ulysses
Uncle Tom's Cabin
Utilitarianism
Utopia
Vanity Fair
Villette
Volpone
Waiting for Godot
Waiting for Lefty
Walden
Walt Whitman: Poems
War and Peace
Washington Square
Weep Not, Child
W. H. Auden: Poems
Where Are You Going, Where Have You Been?
Where the Red Fern Grows
White Fang

47977285R00060

Printed in Poland
by Amazon Fulfillment
Poland Sp. z o.o., Wrocław